About This Book

KU-446-308

A Simple Introduction to Cloud Computing was written for first-time users who need to understand what this recent trend is all about. Cloud-based services run on remote computers rather than on your local device. Users access services either through a browser like Google Chrome or using apps. Most cloud services have versions that run on Windows, Android and iOS.

This book assumes little prior knowledge of Cloud Computing and covers concepts and terminology. In its basic form Cloud Computing is a simple idea that everyone with a computing device can take advantage of and get benefit from.

Cloud Computing changes the way we *consume* computer services. Traditionally we bought our software and storage outright and then bought it all again when it became obsolete or had so many problems we just had to get something new. In the cloud we lease our applications or *apps* as they are now known from a supplier who keeps the software up-to-date and securely stores our data.

The book explores free and paid-for services from the major providers aimed at personal, self-employed and small business users. There are other providers that focus on larger businesses generally known as enterprises. Typically these providers are very expensive and require detailed knowledge of computers and operating systems.

About the Author

Kevin Ryan spent a large part of his career with BBC Monitoring, part of the BBC World Service. After a spell as a radio engineer he lead the newly formed computer engineering team testing and deploying search engines on intranets and the wider internet. Later he worked for the Diocese of Oxford as their Director of ICT and arranged the move of its office applications, e-mail and telephony to the cloud.

He currently runs his own company specializing in internet solutions for small businesses and charities using WordPress, Joomla and a handful of e-commerce packages. He also writes a monthly column for a UK magazine on digital radio and associated technologies.

Books Written by the Same Author

BP566   How to Get Your Website Noticed

BP769   Build Your Own Website with WordPress

Trademarks

All brand and product names used in this book are recognised as trademarks, or registered trademarks, of their respective companies.

Contents

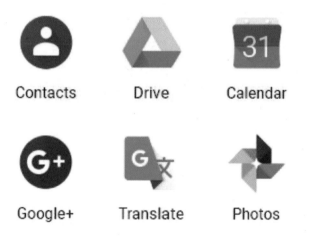

Individual users see a list of apps available in their cloud account like these from Apple (top) and Google Office (Docs).

Dashboard

See relevant insights
about your domain

Users

Add, rename, and
manage users

Admin roles

Add new admins

Device management

Secure corporate data
on devices

Apps

Outlook

OneDrive

Word

Excel

Dynamics
365

Flow

Admin

Security &
Compliance

Business users have more complex portals with management tools. Part of the dashboards from Google G Suite (top) and Microsoft Office 365.

1

Introduction to Cloud Computing

Cloud Computing is a recent computing *invention* that is gaining market share but at its simplest level it is a supplier providing services such as Microsoft Word on their servers that were traditionally installed locally by a business or individual on their own computer.

Before you dismiss the idea out of hand as definitely 'not for me', it is worth knowing what it means once all the jargon is stripped away. I think you might be surprised how many possibilities it provides it terms of saving both time and money.

It is also possible that suppliers may one day leave us with the option of staying with our outdated software that becomes more troublesome with time or signing up to their online services.

A Bit of History

Interestingly, when computing became an essential tool for businesses it was based on locating the computers, either a mainframe (very large) or mid-range device in a central location and connecting users to it using devices called *dumb terminals*, just a screen and keyboard, to use the programs.

The mainframe and the terminals were generally located on the same site or premises because communications links were very expensive. The term *'on premises'* is used by cloud computing providers today as the opposite of *'in the cloud'*. Somewhere in between is the *'hybrid cloud'* that is a mix of the two. The creation of the personal computer changed how business computing worked. The device on the desktop now had its own processing power and memory/disk drives and the central computer , retitled a *fileserver*, became a big storage device *serving up* files and documents.

This is known as the *client-server* model and is widely used today. Clients could either be a *thick client*, i.e. a PC or laptop or a *thin client*, a device not much different to a dumb terminal of old. I think you can see that for many years companies were moving processing power and storage between the desktop and computer room.

This is a simplified history of how computing configurations changed over quite a long period and is not meant to cover all computer installations because the mainframe is still around as are a range of what might be termed dumb terminals. Like the *cloud* they have been given a marketing makeover and some might argue become a bit obscure as to their meaning.

Why the Cloud

The term *cloud computing* became a buzzword for marketing departments and salesmen simply because diagrams (Figure 1.1) that explained the idea always depicted the internet as a fuzzy blob similar to a cloud.

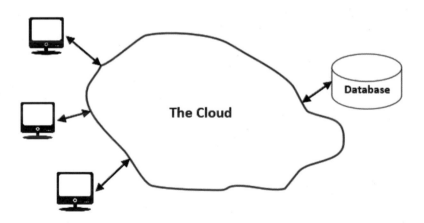

Fig 1.1 A typical cloud-based diagram showing PCs connecting to a remote database provided as a cloud computing service.

The database (Figure 1.1 on page 2) may not be actually in the cloud, even if the marketing people would like you to think that it is, but instead lives on a server in another location and is connected to the internet via an interface just like the PCs.

The Internet Factor

The idea of moving software back to a central location, away from individual PCs and laptops, is back in fashion but it is different now because of the internet, especially as broadband speeds increase. Now familiar software applications can be located anywhere and purchased, or consumed in the suppliers' jargon, like water and electricity.

Something as a Service

Cloud computing is growing year on year and more companies enter the market. Services are under three broad categories. First of all came Software as a Service (SaaS) , Microsoft Office 365 for example, offered in a pay-as-you-use model.

Hardware companies, traditionally associated with physical devices, added concepts such as Platform as a Service (PaaS) that developers can use as an alternative to buying their own hardware and Infrastructure as a Service (IaaS) that is a virtual network.

I will explain exactly what these services can provide in chapter two mainly as background information as it is unlikely that small businesses will need IaaS. You are more likely to use some form of SaaS and perhaps PaaS from time to time for a project.

No Limits to the Cloud

In reality, just about anything be it hardware or software based that is associated with computing can be re-packed as one of these cloud-based services, provided a company's internet connection has enough bandwidth. As first glance this computer revolution may seem something best left to big business but there are benefits for small businesses and the home user.

Not Everything is New

Providers are attaching the cloud computing tag to as many of their services as they can even where a service has not changed in concept. Think of webmail, accessing your e-mail using a browser rather than a mail application and hosting websites on a third party server.

Start to Use the Cloud for Free

The big providers have vast amounts of storage and processing power and many are happy to get your loyalty with offers of free **storage** space. Some of the very generous offers have been scaled back over the years. You can also get 14-day or 30-day trials of other services but beware of forgetting to cancel them in time if you provided billing information.

Small Business User

The cloud is ideal for sharing files especially where there is collaborative working required on proposals and other documents.

Small businesses come in all shapes and sizes ranging from the sole trader through the micro-businesses with a handful of people to a small business with maybe a dozen people.

For a business there are a number of things that might attract you to cloud-based computing especially when you have to upgrade your hardware or software.

1) As it is a pay-as-you-use model you can scale upwards or downwards as your business changes. This may work better than having a large amount of expenditure in one month of the financial year.

2) You don't have to worry about the technical or back-end stuff associated with having your own server as the service provider takes care of this. Cloud computing should also simplify any small network that the business has.

3)   Software updates become a thing of the past as companies like Microsoft do this automatically and you don't need to worry so much about backups as your data has multiple copies in different locations.

4)   The online apps continually save the changes to your document and providers are introducing versions of documents so that you can retrieve revisions from up to 30 days back in time. Very useful if the document has been corrupted.

5)   ICT business continuity risks are considerably reduced as you can now easily operate from another location.

6)   You can usually extend the useful life of PCs and laptops with inexpensive upgrades as much of the processing is carried out remotely.

Other benefits quoted by providers mean more to IT professionals than they do to a business owner.

There are negatives that you need to keep in mind as well.

1)   Small amounts of downtime, usually quoted as high availability may not be what they seem. Note that some seemingly high figures such as 99.9% availability per month equates to seven hours without services per month. Look for closer to 99.99% availability or 30 minutes per month.

2)   You may also need to consider where your data is being stored for legal or ethical reasons.

3)   Your main failure risk is now your internet connection so you should invest in a backup link of some kind, possibly using a 4G mobile connection if you use a landline or vice versa.

4)   The downside of this model is that you don't actually own anything other than your own data and the equipment in your place of work. If this aspect of cloud computing fills you with dread then the *hybrid cloud model* may be of interest.

Personal Users

Reading the previous section might lead you to conclude that cloud computing is all about business users but this is not true. There are services you can set up and use from home and gain the benefits of new software and improved backups for your data. You probably won't ever venture into platforms and infrastructure but access to the latest software and online storage could be cost-effective and time saving solutions.

Owners of Cloud Services

The best of breed providers are companies that you may already be familiar with and usually they provide the widest range of services. They are listed below in no particular order and come with no particular recommendation at this stage in the book.

Google

Google provides cloud services for almost everyone from the personal user to the larger enterprise.

G Suite by Google Cloud

Google Docs

Fig. 1.2 Google has an office suite for personal and business use.

G Suite is aimed at business and Google Docs, that has a subset of the applications is freely available to personal users.

Google Docs has alternatives for most Microsoft Office applications. Google Drive's basic plan comes with 15GB of free storage for personal use and Google is very fair about the type of files that use up that storage. G Suite uses the same apps as Google Docs but with the collaboration features that allows multiple users to work on a document at the same time. This is different to Google Docs where a document is shared.

Microsoft

Fig. 1.3 Office 365 has to have a valid subscription to use either at home for in your business.

Microsoft's Office 365 Business, as the name suggests, is for businesses of all sizes. Office 365 Home is for personal use in two editions. Microsoft also has a free to use Office Online but there are limits as to what you can do with it.

I have Word, Excel and PowerPoint from Office Online on my Windows 10 mobile and they have helped me review or complete a document on more than one occasion.

Amazon

Fig. 1.4 Two apps from Amazon.

Amazon is well known for books, goods and video services and they have a 'reputation' for encouraging us to sign up to **Amazon Prime**. Prime is just the public bit of a large number of services provided by Amazon Web Services.

Hidden away in Prime is **Amazon Drive** that provides both free and paid for storage. Amazon Backup is a useful application to backup files to **Amazon Drive**.

You can subscribe to Amazon Drive without taking out Prime. Like other free storage providers Amazon expects you to use it mainly for photos and videos and has tools and apps to help you do that.

Amazon Web Services is a huge collection of services aimed at the enterprise. They are a collection of Application Interfaces (APIs) that programmers use to make bespoke applications for their business.

AWS is used by many online systems. In my opinion AWS is too complicated for personal or small business use and I would use your valuable time exploring other suppliers. If you are still curious about AWS and particularly the Amazon S3 service there is more information in chapter 12.

Citrix

This is probably a name that you haven't heard before but they are well known to IT professionals. Citrix's product is called ShareFile (Figure 1.5) and offers secure file access and sharing and aims to lure businesses away from what they call 'consumer' grade products. If you need to send documents securely to customers then Citrix is one of the best around. Trials are available so that you can do your own evaluation.

ShareFile

Fig. 1.5 Citrix has very good secure access to files.

Apple

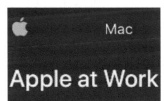

Fig. 1.6 Apple Mac is a successful business machine.

Apple has its iCloud platform and it may not be an obvious solution for business needs. Of itself, the iCloud platform provides synchronization of all iCalendar functions and iCloud Drive updates files across multiple devices.

A strong point of iCloud is that it integrates relatively easily with Microsoft Office. Each release of the Apple operating systems usually means that some apps stop working on devices running older versions of the operating system.

A downside is that iCloud is not available for Android operating system apart from a few third party apps that work with the iCalendar that may be useful.

Dropbox

Dropbox Business

Fig. 1.7 Dropbox is well known supplier of online storage.

Dropbox markets itself for teams and individuals but it also has a business side that, like Citrix, offers enhanced security. Dropbox integrates with Microsoft Office 365 and has Dropbox Paper for teams to work together on ideas.

Box

Fig. 1.8 Box is more than just storage and is adding more tools and apps.

Box is similar in concept to Dropbox in many ways. It integrates with Microsoft Office and Google Docs and has a built in content management system.

Content management is a process that controls file creation and availability. Files are usually named to a convention and stored in a repository reducing the risk that multiple and potentially different copies exist or that files are not stored in personal silos of information.

Other Providers

There are other providers but I will provide the most information on the six companies regarded as the market leaders plus Apple because of its widespread use. These are the companies most likely to stay in the cloud computing business. I will make you aware of the conditions that many of the headline grabbing free storage companies impose on you after tempting you with offers of 50GB of free storage, typically ten times that offered by others.

An internet search will return these suppliers plus other big names like IBM and Axway. These companies are for large businesses with very good ICT support.

Egnyte's team and small office plan has many good features but requires a more in-depth knowledge of IT that is probably not available in a small business. It positions itself as a more adaptable solution than that offered by Box. It may just fit your business needs even though it is not really aimed at the smaller sized company

Fig. 1.9 A good system that is probably not ideal for a small business.

Cloud Services Resellers

In the main, resellers provide access to Microsoft Office or Microsoft Office 365 and are usually available from hosting companies such as 1and1 and 123Reg. Typically they offer combinations of Outlook, Word, Excel and PowerPoint with a generous amount of storage for a monthly cost per user. Their plans need to be read very carefully as you can pay a lot of money for what might be basic storage and hosted e-mail.

Moving to The Cloud

Fig. 1.10 You will become familiar with the cloud upload icon.

The big seven providers have plenty to offer the general user, starting with free plans for individuals. By general user I mean someone who uses a word processor , spreadsheet or slide creation software on a regular basis. For freelancers, a club or association secretary this may be adequate for your needs.

Self Employed and Business Users

If you use software from Microsoft for commercial activity then their licensing terms require you to have the correct subscription plan. Google is happy for you to use Google Docs for your business activities.

The suppliers in the business sector have plans for teams and for the small business where real time collaborative working and business continuity features are more important . Usually you will want a service that works on several operating systems so that your office staff and people in the business can access the same files and documents.

The simplest way is to use one provider like Google or Microsoft but you can integrate services from different suppliers together. For example, if your company has both iPads and Windows PCs then using Apple's iCloud and Microsoft's Office 365 may be the answer you need. If Android is in the mix then I would start with Google first and then Microsoft.

Other Cloud Services

Chapter 14 has an overview of specialist cloud-based services such as accounting and graphic design. It is impossible to cover all possible services available as a cloud-based service but by this stage you will be cloud aware and able to critically appraise what is on offer.

Technical Information

There are several appendices that provide more information of a more technical level so that you can appreciate the knowledge required to administer GSuite and integrate Gmail with an email client.

There are overviews on some of the less well known applications in Microsoft's Office 365 like SharePoint and Yammer, a private social network for your business.

2

Cloud Terminology

Cloud computing is a segment of the IT industry that has its own jargon and terminology. I touched on some of this in chapter one. In this chapter I will cover some of the concepts you are most likely to come across in articles and if you talk to salesmen.

Cloud Types

Fig. 2.1 The Public Cloud is a shared resource with many users.

Fig. 2.2 Private Clouds have many forms.

The cloud providers like to segment cloud computing into three different categories. The one that you are most likely to use is the **Public Cloud** that you access using a web browser. Here all the equipment is owned by a supplier like Microsoft. The public cloud is most likely used in an **on-demand** basis either for a fixed duration (e.g. storage rented per annum) or on a pay-per-use basis where an extra server is used in short bursts. You will be sharing this type of cloud with other users, not a surprise, but providers like to refer to this as **multi-tenancy**.

The second type is the **Private Cloud** used by one business and it might be **in the cloud** or installed in the company's own computer room and is known as **on premises**. The latter is sometimes called an **Internal Cloud** and it might make you wonder why a business would do this.

A company might be security conscious and not want to store its data outside the business. However using the cloud computing model allows for better control and monitoring of who is using computer time.   A multinational operating in several countries could use more servers in locations where costs are cheaper.

Of course, this is all big business stuff. A variation on the private cloud is the **Community Cloud** used by a number of organisations (Figure 2.3) that share common goals or interests. Companies also use community clouds to connect employees, customers and partner organisations.

Fig. 2.3 People sharing a common interest can set up their own cloud .

The final type of cloud is the **Hybrid Cloud** where a public and private cloud can share applications and allow data to move between them.

Someone coined the term **cloud bursting** to describe the situation where extra computing power is supplied by a cloud provider for a short period. This is a typical use of the hybrid model.

Cloud Computing and Hosting

Hosting has been around for a long time and is very similar to cloud computing. Like cloud computing, hosting is scalable, you can ask for more or upgrade your plan and it is multi-tenancy and resilient in that you share the hardware with other users and you may never be aware of problems at the hosting company.

Cloud computing is different in two respects. It is designed as a **pay-per-use model** charging for processing, memory and network access. Companies will undoubtedly have some continuous level of usage. Cloud computing **automatically scales** up or down as usage changes meaning that more servers get added or removed as the demands of users of that particular cloud vary.

Cloud Consumer

The **Cloud Consumer** is you and me. We are called consumers because providers want us to think of computing services like electricity or water. As small scale users we will typically buy into a cloud computing plan of some kind on a subscription basis paying monthly or annually. Our usage is going to be hard to distinguish from traditional hosting .

We will get the most benefit from ease of access to our software applications from any location and fewer headaches by not having to maintain software ourselves.

Fig. 2.4 Some of the Software as a Service (SaaS) applications and business activities available from cloud computing providers.

The SaaS Consumer

Figure 2.4 on page 14 shows services that we might use but there are others. For the individual or personal user **Email**, **Office** and the sharing of files are the most useful options.

A business will also need robust Email and the three main office applications but may have may have some form of **Customer Relationship Management (CRM)** that records contact details of current and potential customers, **Human Resources (HR)** software

that might be as simple as managing holidays and sickness and activities.

Social Networking or Social Media is well known in the form of Facebook and others but you can have your own network in a private space. This can be a handy business tool where staff can share ideas and interact with each other.

Fig. 2.5 Yammer can be your own community cloud.

Microsoft's **Yammer** is a cloud service for staff only or extended to key customers or a wider pool of people that interact with your organisation. You could use Yammer for your own Community Cloud rather than a public social network but you would need a subscription to Microsoft Office 365. There is more information on Yammer in Appendix 4.

Fig. 2.6 Salesforce is a market leader in tools for your sales team.

Salesforce is a well-known provider of services for small businesses. There is a wealth of information on their website, **https://www.salesforce.com** that will help you decide if it might be useful for your business. The Salesforce **Sales Cloud Essentials** lets you track all your interactions with your customers in a single app. You use **Service Cloud Essentials ,** as the name suggests, to manage how you support your customers.

The IaaS Consumer

Grouped under the broad category of IaaS are **Hosting** for websites that will use up **Storage**, memory and disks, and runs on a **Central Processing Unit (CPU)** or processor. As an individual or small business you buy these as a fixed package and can only trade up or down by buying a different hosting plan. Larger businesses burst up and scale down almost in real time like you consume electricity and there are metering charges for each element. Amazon's AWS service, more on this cloud service in chapter 12, provides this type of scalable hosting to many well known companies who use it to build their websites.

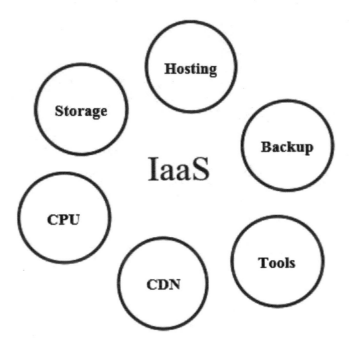

Fig. 2.7 IaaS is a set of strange bedfellows some of which could be included in the SaaS family of cloud services.

Backup covers both data generated and stored in the cloud and data you might upload from your devices, such as a backup from an iPad. If you start to use GSuite or Office 365 then you will have to learn administrative **Tools** to manage your users.

A new concept is a **Content Delivery Network (CDN)** that consists of servers in different locations so that clients can access the one nearest to them.   It is something worth knowing about even though you are unlikely to implement it in practice.

The PaaS Consumer

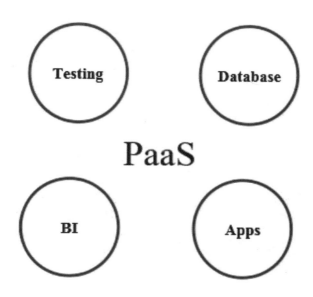

Figure 2.8 Platform as a Service (PaaS) is primarily a development and testing facility for new applications.

The most interesting member of this family is **Business Intelligence (BI)** as it could well be under the SaaS umbrella. BI provides businesses with performance data usually in a visual form called dashboards.

Business Intelligence (BI) software has been around for decades but is was difficult to implement correctly mainly because it was hard to connect to many different systems to gather the data. With many more sources online the data gathering is easier but it still requires skilled staff to extract it from databases and spreadsheets and create meaningful results called dashboards for managers to pore over.

Microsoft has BI tools built into its Dynamics 365 that gathers data from sales, services , finance and operations to streamline business processes, provide insights on customers and identify areas for growth.

Cloud Computing Glossary

There are several comprehensive glossaries on the internet if you feel you need to know more. You will find that that most glossaries have many more entries in their cloud computing dictionary that I have covered in this chapter but I think I have covered the essentials. The industry is evolving so the list of terms and definitions will grow.

The Future

All the forecasters predict that cloud computing will grow rapidly in the next ten years with most predictions using estimated expenditure on the technology to underline their thinking. In that period cloud computing will become the norm through the education of new users and suppliers offering few traditional alternatives.

Others foresee that one of those regular shifts in IT will happen sooner or later and the emphasis will move back to the user and moving data and applications back to company premises.

My own view is that whatever the big companies decide the individual user will continue with cloud computing because it is so convenient and trouble free. Once you experience it for yourself I think you will see just how useful it is.

3

Moving to the Cloud

Cloud Computing will grip your imagination as you discover its possibilities. Your instinct is to rush ahead and experience the services the suppliers have to offer. There is nothing wrong with this as you can sign up for trials without any financial commitment.

- 🖥 Desktop
- ⬆ Recent Places
- ⬇ Downloads
- Google Drive
- ☘ Dropbox
- Box Sync
- ☁ OneDrive
- ❀ iCloud Photos
- ☁ iCloud Drive
- ⚑ Amazon Drive

Fig. 3.1 The six main cloud players are listed here in Favorites in Explorer in Windows 7.

At some point you have to take these steps as you have to decide if you want to work the cloud way. The various online services will all co-exist without interaction (Figure 3.1) because they are just folders but they will load a piece of software to connect to them and this will slow down your PC, especially at startup.

I would caution you not to rush ahead and start moving lots of documents and photos online. I make copies of a few files and use these to learn how to use each service because they all vary.

It is unlikely that you will lose data as a result of an unreliable service but the documentation is never that clear. The danger comes from you thinking you have done something wrong and trying to prematurely stop the copying of files and photos. Typical examples are realising that your documents are being deleted from your local device or that you have selected a huge amount of data to copy to the cloud.

Start small, work incrementally and understand what has happened on your device and in the cloud. Using the cloud is a skill and you learn about it by doing.

Be Diligent

First of all check any eye-catching free offers carefully because the headline features may be for a trial period only and you might have to do a lot of free marketing for the provider to retain any benefits. All these companies want you to buy a subscription and they do everything to encourage you to do this.

I recommend that you double check if you could affect software already installed on your device. The risk is greater for Windows based devices like PCs and laptops and in some cases it might need a system restore to uninstall what becomes unwanted software.

For example, when it was launched I wanted to see what Office 2016 was like to use and I signed up for an extended free trial. Fortunately, I used my laptop rather than my business critical desktop because the Microsoft installer updated my Office 2007 software leaving me with no easy way to get it back other than a system restore. If you purchase a subscription from Microsoft then software will be installed on your PC or laptop.

Definitions

In this chapter I use the term **Storage** to cover all forms of cloud-based storage and **Office Online** to mean a suite of applications that includes word processing, spreadsheets, presentations, email and messaging. I use this term in a supplier independent way and it applies to Microsoft, Google, Apple, etc.

Three applications form the core of every office suite, whether it comes from Microsoft of not. They are a word processor to create documents, a spreadsheet to handle numbers, and an application to create presentations, storyboards and dashboards .

Depending on the suite, and in some cases depending on which version of a suite you choose, you also get an email and calendar app, a database manager, PDF editing software, a note-taking app, web page maker and any of a dozen miscellaneous apps and services ranging from web conferencing through form-building.

A free-to-use version of an Office Online suite will usually use a slightly different version of the software with fewer functions. The free version may not be easy to adapt to foster working together in teams on projects or working jointly on documents in real-time. You can work around this but it is tedious.

Storage Only

Fig. 3.2 CloudPro is a useful source of information on cloud storage.

There are many cloud storage providers and an online search should provide a recent review of the top ten or fifteen providers at that point in time. It is best to use trusted reviews from sources like PC Magazine **(http://uk.pcmag.com)**, the Tech Advisor website **(www.techadvisor.co.uk)** or CloudPro **(http://www.cloudpro.co)** as shown in Figure 3.2.

Combining the results from these two sources will give you some twenty providers to choose from and I usually shortlist down to names that feature in each list. The reviews will include both business and personal needs where the requirements are quite different.

Fig. 3.3 Google Drive is easy to set up and use

Business needs can include things like legal compliance requirements, support for team folders, authenticated logins and data encryption.

Personal users may be more concerned with the amount of storage provided, basic sharing of files and folders and ease of use. Business users normally want more functionality in their applications.

Big Names

I consider Amazon, Google, Microsoft, Dropbox, Apple and Box as the big six in the personal market. Even though they can be adapted for business I would not consider using Amazon and Apple for commercial activity. These six providers are covered in more detail later in chapters four through twelve.

Dropbox and Box are more interested in the business market and Dropbox works on more operating systems than anyone else. Amazon also provides generous free storage with no frills that is useful on occasion. A comparison , Figure 3.4, shows Google as the most generous free storage provider, followed by Box.   Note that free storage plans are aimed at the personal user .

Provider	Free Storage	Personal	Business
Amazon	5GB	Amazon Drive	AWS
Box	10GB	Box	4 separate plans
Dropbox	2GB	Dropbox	3 plans from Dropbox for Business.
Google	15GB	Google Drive	GSuite
Apple iCloud	5GB	iCloud	Apple at Work
Microsoft	5GB	OneDrive	OneDrive for Business

Fig. 3.4 A comparison of free personal storage plans offered by well known providers. Businesses are expected to buy a subscription.

Other Providers

There are many other providers of cloud storage that may prompt you to do some additional research. The examples included here are to alert you to some of the marketing devices in this segment of the market and not to recommend any particular vendor.

MEGA
THE PRIVACY COMPANY

Fig. 3.5 MEGA's free account offers a generous amount of storage to start with but watch out for others reselling MEGA services as their own product.

FREE

0.00 €

50 GB ★
STORAGE

Limited
TRANSFER

Fig. 3.6 MEGA's free account limits as advertised.

MEGA

New providers appear on a regular basis and some allow you to earn extra storage by linking them to your social media accounts and promoting them to your friends. Providers add new features from time to time.

Typically they add basic document editing, email, messaging and video calls.

The amount of storage provided under the various plans offered by providers varies considerably. Again, be cautious of what is on offer and if it seems to be too good to be true then in probably is. If you like the offer then do some research and check other users' comments in independent forums.

In 2018, the best free account was from a New Zealand company called MEGA (http://mega.nz) (Figure 3.5) whose headline offering was an extremely generous 50GB of free storage as shown in Figure 3.6.

On the plus side, MEGA takes security very seriously and your data in encrypted at every stage but the onus is on the user to maintain that level of security. The user password is the encryption key or seed and there is no password recovery method. MEGA warns you about this at every step. You also have to accept several pages of terms and conditions before gaining access to their services.

There is the need to agree to participate in their achievements program. You only find out what this is when you sign-up for the Free Account (Figure 3.5 on page 23) and under the Achievements tab in your user account find that the free storage is really made up of a 15GB base quota plus 35GB that you have for 30 days.

You can earn extensions though other actions or achievements but all time out after either 180 or 365 days. Of course, all of this is to get you to purchase a paid-for plan. Some time after I set up my MEGA account I received an e-mail telling me that I had lost some of my benefits. Another recent entrant called pCloud also has incentive schemes to earn extra storage. MEGA's base quota is generous but Google Drive also gives you 15GB of storage in their free account without any of these loyalty complications.

Remember that if you are storing documents then a few Gigabytes may be enough for your needs. Photographs and videos will quickly eat up your storage and you will need to either use multiple providers or a paid-for plan.

BigMind Lifetime Storage

Fig. 3.7 Zoolz introduced the concept of Lifetime Storage.

BigMind, originally Zoolz, came to prominence in 2018 with the slogan of *Lifetime Storage*. It has a catch in that home users can only access their data with a two to fivehour delay. Called **Cold Storage,** the service is intended for long term backups. They also offer **Hot Storage** that gives you instant access.

FREE

5 GB
Great for personal use

1 User

3 Computers

2 Mobile/Tablets Devices

SD Video Streaming

No Backup Limitations

1 External Drive

No Support

Fig. 3.8 Individuals get 5GB of storage but business users are offered 10GB.

Fig. 3.9 The intelligent cloud lets you search for your content in various ways.

The company has many other offerings such as **Instant Vault** and its **Intelligent Cloud** for both home and business use that searches for your content by identifying objects within images. For example, you could search for 'cars', 'flowers', etc.

It also lets you stream your home videos in Standard Definition (SD) quality without buffering and the free offering is 5GB. BigMind offers **Personal**, **Family** and **Family Plus** plans starting around £75 per annum and the Family Plus plan upgrades the video quality to High Definition (HD). Bear in mind that this may stretch your broadband to the limit and you ideally need a fibre based broadband plan with unlimited usage.

BigMind for Business

The intelligent cloud (Figure 3.9) concept for business has other niche products for business sectors. The company targets Healthcare, Legal, Accounting, Photographers, Dental, CCTV based security and many more. **https://intelli.zoolz.co.uk/zoolz-in-action/.** The Free Business account comes with 10GB of storage. You can't upgrade a Home account to a Business one as they are separate product streams. There are versions for iOS, macOS, Windows and Android.

Storage and Basic Office (Personal)

If you want a cloud computing solution that gives you both a reasonable amount of storage and applications to carry out the creation of most kinds of basic documents then look at Apple, Google and Microsoft.

Microsoft OneDrive	Google Drive	Apple iCloud
Word Online to create documents.	Google Docs	Pages
Excel Online for financial work .	Google Sheets	Numbers
5 GB Free Storage for documents, photos, etc.	15 GB Free Storage, photos are separate	5 GB that is divided into backups, photos and documents.
PowerPoint Online to make presentations.	Google Slides	Keynote
OneNote to capture screen clippings, snippets of data, etc.	Keep	Notes
Outlook to edit, send and read e-mails.	Gmail	Mail, Calendar, Reminders
Skype for one-to-one communication	Hangouts	Facetime

Fig 3.10 A short comparison between Microsoft , Apple and Google and the features in their free packages for the individual.

Microsoft Office

Microsoft Office, whether installed as standalone software or as part of the subscription-based Office 365 service, is the most popular office suite. Nearly all other office online providers try to be compatible with Microsoft Office and let you save or download documents in Office's file formats.

Office for the Mac includes slightly different versions of Word, Excel, PowerPoint, Outlook, and OneNote, but leaves out the Access database and Publisher. When you buy Microsoft Office, for either Windows or the Mac, you get the latest version. It gets minor updates from Windows Update.

When you subscribe to Office 365, your copies of the office apps are automatically updated with new features , and you don't have to pay extra when the current Office 2016 apps get replaced by an overhauled new version in the future.

By default Microsoft's Online Office apps try to save documents in Microsoft OneDrive that then creates synchronized copies of your documents both on your hard disk and in the cloud, so you can edit them with your desktop-based apps even when you're offline. Microsoft makes it easy to edit and access your documents either online through a browser or locally through a desktop app, and it's one of Office's major advantages.

File Formats

If you're ready to switch from Microsoft Office, or if you simply want an alternative, you'll need to be prepared to deal with the inconvenience of using non-Microsoft document formats in an Office-centric world. The only document formats that everyone can handle are Microsoft's Word and Excel formats, and you can set up your non-Microsoft apps to save in those formats. If you only share documents within an organization that has standardized on non-Microsoft formats, this won't be an issue, but it will be an issue if you send documents to anyone outside.

Microsoft Office Alternatives

The widespread use of Microsoft Office doesn't mean that it is necessarily the best suite for your specific purposes as you probably won't use many of its advanced features.   One thing that all of today's suites have in common is that their core apps share functionality. For example, the drawing tools in the presentation app are typically also available in reduced form in the word processor and spreadsheet. Also, the core apps typically share a similar interface, so you can move from one to the other without having to learn where to find basic features.

Google

Google's paid-for GSuite and the free Google Docs, Sheets, and Slides keeps all your documents on Google Drive, which may be a disadvantage if you want the editing power of a desktop app like Word or Excel. You can download Google's documents in standard formats like those used by Microsoft Office or LibreOffice, but the originals are always in the cloud.

Google's apps include Docs, Sheets, Slides, all available from a menu that appears at the upper right of Google's home page when you're signed into any Google account. The same menu includes all of Google's free services such as Gmail, and Google Drive. The commercial G Suite has voice and video conferencing and a variety of account management services; higher-priced subscriptions include auditing and data-retention features.

Google operates only in the cloud, accessible via a web browser or Android/iOS apps, not via desktop-based programs, and you can only edit your Google documents when you're online.

There is an offline browsing feature available through the **Chrome** browser, but only if you've already installed an offline-editing add-in for Chrome. Prior to using this feature you need to mark your documents in Google Drive as being available offline and give Drive time to create local copies.

iWork from Apple

Apple's office apps are marketed on Apple's website as iWork, but you won't find a suite of that name to download because they are separate apps.

Fig 3. 11 Some of the Apple iWork apps.

The Pages word processor, Numbers spreadsheets apps, and Keynote presentation app are visually impressive but may not have the features you want. However, if you want to open an iWork document under Windows, Android, or Linux, you'll need to access it through a browser and if you had revision-tracking turned on in your Numbers document, may find that you can only view it, not edit it, in the browser interface.

Apple's apps can export and import files in Microsoft's and LibreOffice's format, but there's no Windows or Linux app that can open iWork documents in their own format. Apple's elegance and simplicity may be enough to make up for this if you simply use products from Apple, and Numbers has the distinction of being the only current spreadsheet app that breaks the Excel mould by letting you create multiple tables on the same sheet.

Kingsoft WPS

Fig. 3.12 WPS has a free Windows version.

WPS Office 2016 includes the three main applications you expect to find in an office suite. There are four versions available.

1G free storage space for WPS user

Get It

Fig. 3.13 It is not a large amount of cloud storage but WPS finally became cloud aware in 2018.

The free version has advertisements every now and then but they tend not to be that intrusive. The Premium version removes these adverts and is not that expensive at £25 per annum, the service is priced in US dollars so this can vary. The amount of cloud storage stays at 1GB no matter which plan you choose.

Kingsoft Office's seven day History Service will store your previous documents. Thus the documents can be recovered even in case of having to reinstall the software or if you lose your device. In addition, the documents can be synchronized to your mobile phone, PC and tablet computer. You will have access to them at any time wherever you are.

Note that Kingsoft WPS sets itself as the default programme for many file types on a Windows device including files using the PDF format. You will have to manually change each entry if you are unhappy with that.

Kingsoft WPS is available on iOS as WPS Office and as WPS Office + PDF for Android. These versions include guides and a PDF Reader, PDF Editor and Creator.   WPS works with both Microsoft Office and Google Docs formats.

Corel Office

I include WordPerfect for completeness even though there is little sign that Corel is going to add cloud computing functionality to the product.

Corel Office is made up of the WordPerfect word processor, Quattro Pro spreadsheet program , presentations slideshow creator Lightning, a digital notebook and AfterShot 2 RAW photo-editing software

LibreOffice

Fig. 3.14 LibreOffice is starting to embrace cloud computing.

Fig. 3.15 Google Drive works with LibreOffice.

Until release 6 LibreOffice was only a desktop application, composed of a word processor called Writer, a spreadsheet called Calc, a presentation app called Impress, a vector-graphics app called Draw, a separate math module called Math, a separate charting module called Charts, and a database manager called Base.

Users in your organization can still only use LibreOffice by launching its desktop apps. You can't use it through a browser, and you can't use it through a mobile app. These limitations come with security advantages. Another advantage is that LibreOffice looks and feels a lot like older versions of Microsoft Office, before Microsoft replaced the old menu-and-toolbar interface with the Ribbon interface introduced with Office 2007.

LibreOffice can access files on Google Drive and that works quite well (Figure 3.15). Accessing OneDrive was a problem and Microsoft's security may prevent this from ever happening.

LibreOffice supports third party extensions but cloud storage access is not being developed very quickly and the only available extension uses a separate connection service.

OpenOffice

Fig. 3.16 OpenOffice shares a common origin with LibreOffice.

This product is very similar to LibreOffice and that is because they share a common root. They diverged a few years ago and each group now develops their office suites separately. OpenOffice (Figure 3.16) has a single extension, via a third party portal, to access the cloud which is a limiting factor. Like LibreOffice there is little indication that cloud computing access will be improved in the short term.

Fig. 3.17 Part of the OpenOffice Presentation tool bars.

OpenOffice may be of interest to you if you like a screen layout similar to older versions of Microsoft Office as OpenOffice hasn't changed the layout very much (Figure 3.17) in the last decade.

Options to Consider

There are factors common to both personal and business users that may determine how you start to adopt cloud computing. You probably have computer equipment already and it makes sense to start with the cloud services provided with that operating system. If you use an iPad with iOS I would use iCloud as a starting point, Windows users should start with OneDrive and Android users should start with Google Drive. If you have a mixed economy of equipment OneDrive or Google Drive are good starting points. Having cloud storage also gives you a suite of office applications.

The second consideration is the security of you data and whether you feel happier with using a big company like Google or Apple rather than a relatively new entrant to the market. The final issue may be one of your available budget and how much you are willing to spend expanding the free storage.

Business Considerations

When you choose an office suite, are you choosing for yourself or your whole organization? If you're self employed, choosing for yourself, use whatever feels most comfortable, but if you choose anything other than Microsoft Office, and you plan to send your files to other people, be prepared to set up your suite to export files in the standard Microsoft formats that almost everyone else expects.

If you're choosing for a small business then matters get more complicated. Most of your colleagues are probably going to be familiar with Microsoft Office , but it has two disadvantages: the desktop apps cost significant money, and you may have strong reasons to avoid proprietary software.

If you insist on open-source software, then LibreOffice or WPS office are your only serious choices, but LibreOffice suffers from a clunky interface with confusing menus and WPS Office has limited cloud storage.

If you want free software, and you only use a Mac, then you can use the free copies of Apple's apps that come with your machine. If you're content with cloud-only software, then Google's apps are powerful and improving all the time.

Microsoft Office and its subscription-based version, Office 365, clearly lead the field, but it is not for everyone. Unfortunately, there's no clear preference among the Office alternatives, but you can test all of them , Office itself, in free or trial versions. All the Office apps are mature, widely used, and heavily tested, and whichever one you choose, you can't go far wrong.

4

Google Docs

My aim in this chapter is to give you a broad introduction to Google Office commonly referred to as Google Docs (Figure 4.1). There are many apps and it is not possible to cover them in great detail. Google Docs is available to anyone with a Google account or Google Gmail account. If you want to read more about this cloud service go to **https://www. google.com/docs/about/** and scroll through the documentation.

Docs

Sheets

Slides

Fig. 4.1 Google's three office applications available for free.

You need to select the application from the top menu bar to read about that piece of software. If you want to try the system then click on the link **Go To Google Docs**. All these apps install or activate an extension in Chrome on a Windows desktop.

Google Docs

Docs is a word processor compatible with Word documents and it has a number of add-ons or extensions listed under business, education, productivity, social and communication and utilities categories, most of which are free to use, but need permissions to access your Google Docs data.

Google Sheets

Sheets works with Microsoft Excel files and has many add-ons in the same categories as Google Docs. It's most compelling feature are the alternative chart options that are standard and not easily achievable in Microsoft Excel.

Google Slides

Slides works with Microsoft PowerPoint presentations and has the fewest add-ons. It interfaces with Chromecast, Hangouts and Airplay. **Chromecast** is Google's TV device and can be used to stream a presentations via Wi-Fi to a large screen TV. This is Google's alternative to plugging a laptop via a cable connected to the TV. **Airplay** is the Apple equivalent. **Hangouts** is Google's instant message, group chat and audio/video calling application.

Google Forms

Forms, as the name suggests, is used to create forms for surveys, event registration and creating a poll. The forms are either distributed via social media or embedded in a web page and the results can be collated in Google Sheets. Forms is separate to the other three apps and you have to login to it directly.

Getting a Google Account

One account is all you need

One free account gets you into everything Google.

Fig. 4.2 Use a single Google account to access all of their services.

You need to set up your credentials on Google Docs when you use it for the first time and after that it will log you in automatically. You can obtain a Google account (Figure 4.2) at **https:// accounts.google.com**. You can register for a Gmail e-mail address or use your current non-Google e-mail address, although that does cause a few frustrations with Google services.

Using Google Docs

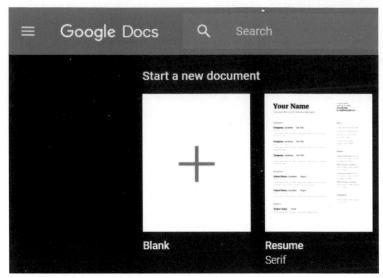

The URL for Google Docs is **https://docs.google.com** or you can
just login to your Google account and select Docs from the general
menu.

When Docs opens for the first time you get a few template options
starting with a blank document (Figure 4.3) and a small selection of
suggested templates.   The
screen is uncluttered   with a
couple of hotspots.

Fig. 4.4 Template Gallery controls in   The Template Gallery has an
Google Docs.   Up/Down symbol (Figure 4.4)
that   opens   many   more
templates and a three vertical dots settings symbol that switches
them off altogether. To get the templates back go to the menu
symbol, click on Settings and tick the box to restore them.

Your First Document

Untitled document

File   Edit   View   Insert   Format   Tools   Table   Add-ons   Help

🖶 ↶ ↷ ⏱   100% ▾   **Normal text** ▾   Arial   ▾

Fig. 4.5 Part of the editing screen for documents showing the menu bar at the top and a toolbar underneath it.

Select the Blank template and the screen shown in Figure 4.5 opens. Compared to Microsoft Word this is a minimal screen although if you have used any word

processor before then the menu bar has familiar entries. The only available toolbar is visible and you hide the menu bar using the up-arrow control next to the Editing option. There are three ways of working. **Editing** (Figure

Fig. 4.6 Editing mode control and menu bar toggle option.

4.6) is for the creation of new documents, **Suggesting** is to suggest edits to the original creator and **Read and Print** is the view or read-only mode.

Working with File Formats

Microsoft formats for documents (.doc and .docx), spreadsheets (.xls and .xlsx) and slides (.ppt and .pptx) are the best portable file formats available as other software suppliers usually ensure compatibility with it. The alternative is to use the OpenDocument format (.odt) developed by OpenOffice and also used by LibreOffice.

Word will use the .odt format but you will lose some Word features such as comments, tracking changes, large size tables although this is unlikely to be a great issue and document protection that may cause a few headaches.

Open a file

My Drive   Shared with Me   Starred   Recent   Upload

Documents ✖   ▾   🔍

Folders

📁   Documents

Fig. 4.7 Use the Upload menu entry to move files from your device into Google Docs that stores them in Google Drive.

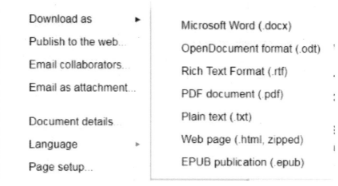

Download as	▶	Microsoft Word (.docx)
Publish to the web...		OpenDocument format (.odt)
Email collaborators..		Rich Text Format (.rtf)
Email as attachment...		PDF document (.pdf)
Document details		Plain text (.txt)
Language	▶	Web page (.html, zipped)
Page setup...		EPUB publication (.epub)

Fig. 4.8 The download option has commonly used formats also available in the Email as attachment menu

It is easy to convert .doc and .docx files to .gdoc, you simply upload the Word document , via the **Open a file** menu (Figure 4.7) to the Google Docs app. To save your document back to Word select the Download option located in the File Menu as shown in Figure 4.8. Note that you are unable to download a file in the native .gdoc format. Even if you chose the **Email as Attachment** option the same formats are available. Of course, there is no absolute reason to use the .gdoc format outside of Google Drive.

Brochure

File   Edit   View   Insert   Format   Tools   Add-ons

Fig. 4.9 The top-level menu of Google Docs. Click on Add-ons to find extensions.

There are several add-ons (Figure 4.9) available in five categories. The list offered to you changes each time you access the extension store, something you also experience with Google's search engine.

The add-on store operates in a similar way to Google Chrome and you have to hover over most of the entries to check how highly, or not, other users scored them.

There are not many add-ons rated at four or five stars and some do not have any rating at all. It is a question of seeing something that interests you and that you need , trying it and taking it from there. You will probably be asked to grant the add-on permissions including connecting to a third party service (Figure 4.10).

PandaDoc **wants to**

●   View and manage documents that this application has been installed in

     Display and run third-party web content in prompts and sidebars inside Google applications

     Connect to an external service

Fig. 4.10 PandaDoc asks for additional permissions that you probably don't want to give.

Using Add-Ons

There are numerous extensions available but I would caution you to proceed carefully mainly because of security concerns. Google

Docs has basic versions of many useful tools such as drawing shapes and inserting tables so you may not need to use any add-ins.   Explore the three main apps first of all before diving into the extensions. In my opinion most of them are poor quality.

Fig. 4.11 The horizontal bars is your route to the main menu. If any other symbol is visible then you are in a sub-menu

My Drive ▾

Folders

📁   **Documents**

Files

🗓   2017 Calendar

Fig. 4.12 Top level view of your folders.

Sharing Documents

Sharing, allowing others to have access to a limited number of documents is straightforward with Google Docs and the application will let you see your folder structure by opening the blue menu (Figure 4.11) and looking in Drive (Figure 4.12). This provides similar functions as those in Windows Explorer and you should explore what each of the down arrows do to learn where the options are located.

Unless you add folders then all the files you create are stored at the top level.

Clicking on the down arrow next to My Drive (Figure 4.12) allows you to **Create a New Folder**, **Upload Files** or **Upload a Folder**.

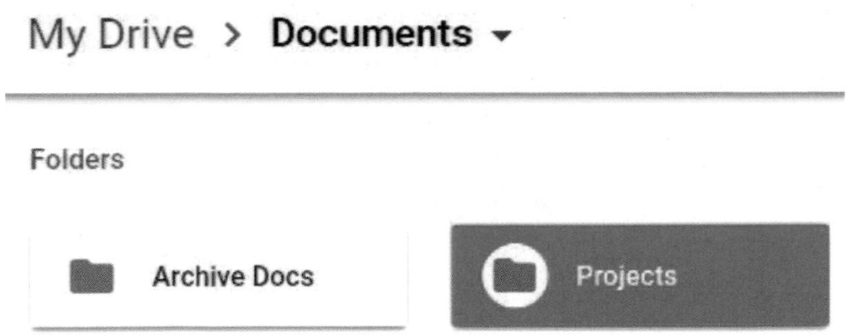

My Drive > **Documents** ▾

Folders

🗂 Archive Docs	⬜ Projects

Fig 4.13 Create sub-folders below Documents by selecting the down arrow and then clicking on Add Folder.

You can add sub-folders to each folder (Figure 4.13) to create a nested structure. To do this you need to be in the parent folder and then click on the down arrow next to that folder's name to get the **New Folder** option.

Link sharing

🌐 **On** – Public on the web
Anyone on the Internet can find and access this. No sign-in required.

👥 **On** – Anyone with the link
Anyone who has the link can access. No sign-in required.

👤 **Off** – Specific people
Shared with specific people.

Fig. 4.14 Sharing a folder is done using links to the URL of the folder within the larger Google Drive. You can only chose one option.

Right Clicking on the folder itself gives you several other options including **Share** (Figure 4.14) **, Download , Remove, Rename and Move**. You can also colour code your folders and add a star to help you find them again by putting 'starred' into the search box.

My Drive > Documents > **Projects** ▾ 👥

Fig. 4.15 The owner can check access to this folder by hovering over the people icon.

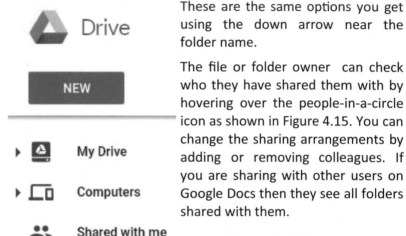

These are the same options you get using the down arrow near the folder name.

The file or folder owner can check who they have shared them with by hovering over the people-in-a-circle icon as shown in Figure 4.15. You can change the sharing arrangements by adding or removing colleagues. If you are sharing with other users on Google Docs then they see all folders shared with them.

Fig. 4.16 Shared with me on the main Drive menu.

Using the main menu entry of **Shared with me** (Figure 4.16) brings up a list of files and folders that other people shared with you as shown in Figure 4.17. If you share with specific people Google assumes they have a login to Drive and will invite them to create a Google account. Sharing outside of Google requires sending a link to them so avoiding the need for a login.

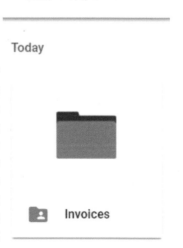

Shared with me

Today

Invoices

Fig. 4.17 Folders shared with me.

Using Google Sheets

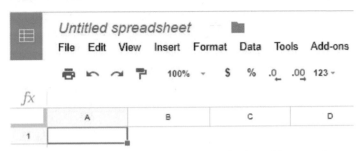

Fig. 4.18 The Sheets opening screen is laid out like Google Docs with a top menu bar with a toolbar underneath..

The Sheets app has a familiar spreadsheet layout (Figure 4.18)and includes some useful templates such as a sample invoice and a project Gantt chart. Sheets can **Sort** data, apply **Filters**, create **Pivot Tables** and insert **Charts** (Figure 4.19), some of which are not easily done in Excel. Sheets will open .xlsx, .xls and .csv files uploaded from your PC and download work sheets in .xlsx, .pdf or .odt formats. The latter is the Open Documents format that is used by LibreOffice and other open source suites.

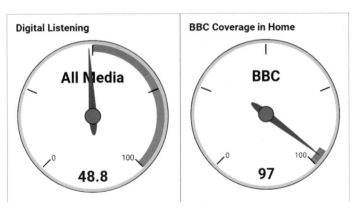

Fig. 4.19 A gauge chart created in Sheets using settings available in the chart dialogue.

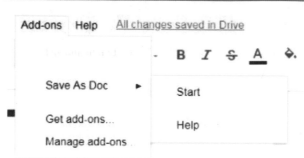

Google Sheets also has many extensions such as Save As Doc that converts some or all of the spreadsheet to a document file. Add-ons are available under a single tab as shown in Figure 4.20.

Fig. 4.20 Convert your spreadsheet to a document using the Save As Doc add-on.

Updates

Google Sheets is part of the commercial GSuite plan from Google and gets frequent updates that become available in the free versions. The updates are always flagged clearly in a bright blue NEW box.

One of the most recent ones was the recording of macros as shown in Figure 4.21.

If you need to format new data imports or create the same chart in several sheets every month or quarter then repeating the same steps manually can take hours, but the Sheets macro recorder lets you record those actions and play them back on command without having to write any code.

Fig. 4.21 Macros lets you store a list of commands to work on cells in the spreadsheet.

Using Google Slides

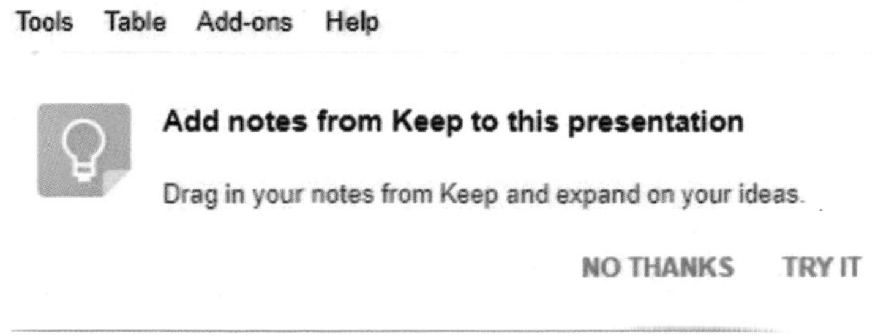

Tools   Table   Add-ons   Help

 Add notes from Keep to this presentation

Drag in your notes from Keep and expand on your ideas.

NO THANKS   TRY IT

Fig. 4.22 On first usage Slides prompts you to use Google Keep, a clippings store, screen capture and note taking app.

Slides is not as rich in features as PowerPoint but you can still create stunning presentations with it. **Google Keep** appears when you open Slides and clicking on **TRY IT** adds a sidebar to keep notes. If you close the app it disappears and if you like this idea of a giant online clipboard then depending on your device you either install it as a Chrome extension or download the app for Android or iOS.

☆ 🗐 💡 ⋮

Fig. 4.23 The Google Keep symbol in Chrome is like a lightbulb

On a Windows device Chrome will have a Keep Icon on the Chrome menu bar (Figure 4.23). You access your notes at **keep.google.com**.

In Google Slides and Google Docs the Keep notepad is accessible via the Tools menu (Figure 4.24). It is not available in Google Sheets, probably because it would not be that useful. Slides can create very good presentations and they could be much better if some more of the add-ons delivered all they promised and had good help files.

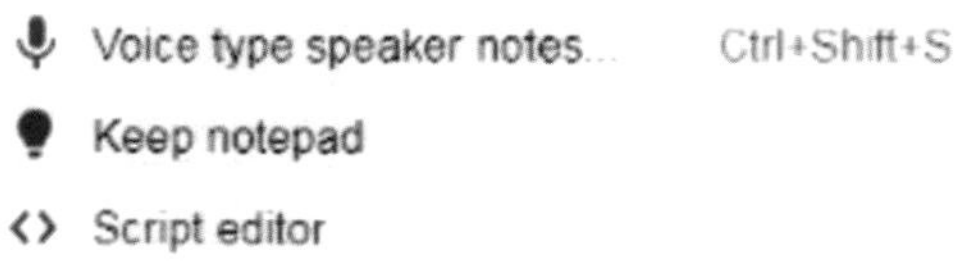

🎤 Voice type speaker notes   Ctrl+Shift+S

💡 Keep notepad

<> Script editor

Fig. 4.24 The Keep notepad as it appears in the Google Slides menu.

Background...   Layout ⌄   Theme...   Transition...

Fig.4.25 The lower part of the Google Slides menu bar.

Figure 4.25 shows part of the lower menu bar where you can **Add Comments**, change the **Background**, select a different **Layout** for each page, change the overall **Theme** and how the pages in the slide deck transition form one to the other when you run the slide show.

Slides will insert the usual range of things including charts created in Google Sheets. Slides has a thing called **Word Art** (Figure 4.26) that is not connected to Microsoft Word. Typing letters into the input box creates a logo like version of the word.

Fig. 4.26 Word Art inserts a stylized version of the words typed into a text box.

Google Drive Storage

If you use Google Docs you might have noticed that files created in the three main apps do not use up any storage and the 15GB available is only used up when you upload files to My Drive. Items in the Trash, Gmail messages and photos in their original size, not processed by Google, all take up space. This is a reasonable approach and by using Google apps you can work with 15GB.

Working Offline

Google Docs Offline

Get things done offline with the Google Docs family of products.

DETAILS   REMOVE

Fig. 4.27 The Google Docs Offline extension is installed in Chrome.

Google has an option in the Google Drive Settings to set up your device to work offline and provide access to files created in Google apps using the Chrome browser (Figure 4.27).

This feature seems to need the Backup and Sync app installed on your PC for reliable operation. In My Drive and on an iOS or Android device there is an option in the settings for each file to make it available offline. You will find Backup and Sync apps in both app stores but they are not created by Google so be careful using them.

Google Backup & Sync for Windows

There have been many software applications for synchronizing local copies of files with those stored centrally although many did not work reliably. Employees who worked away from the office update and create new documents on the move and these changes are copied automatically to the business server when they re-join their devices to the office network.

This new tool replaces the existing Google Photos desktop uploader and Drive for iOS, Android and Windows and backs up files and photos safely in Google Drive and Google Photos.

Backup & Sync Setup

The software is available under Settings in Google Drive or at **https://www.google.com/drive/download/backup-and-sync/**.

The installation is fast but the application does not then launch automatically as you would expect. You should find a new entry in the Start Menu on your Windows desktop.

Now that the Backup and Sync tool is installed on your computer, it's time to set it up. When you launch the app, the first thing you'll have to do is sign in to your Google account. Next you select the folders on your computer that you want to continually back up to Drive. What this means is that all the files in the selected folders will be moved to the cloud and any files and folders on Google Drive will be available in a folder called Google Drive that is visible in Windows Explorer.

Choose folders from your computer to continuously back up to Google Drive

Find them in the "Computers" tab at drive.google.com

Fig. 4.28 The Backup and Sync app guides you through the process.

Once the relationship is set up then as soon as you add a new file to one of the desktop device folders, it will be moved to Drive automatically. If you look in Google Drive via Windows Explorer you won't see any reference to your local files.

You can only check the status of your files by logging into My Drive and if you want other individuals to have access then you must add share permissions. You can choose to back up only a few folders you have on your computer or all of them, essentially backing up your entire computer.

However, it's worth pointing out that your Google account only has 15 GB of free storage, which is shared between Photos, Gmail, and Drive.

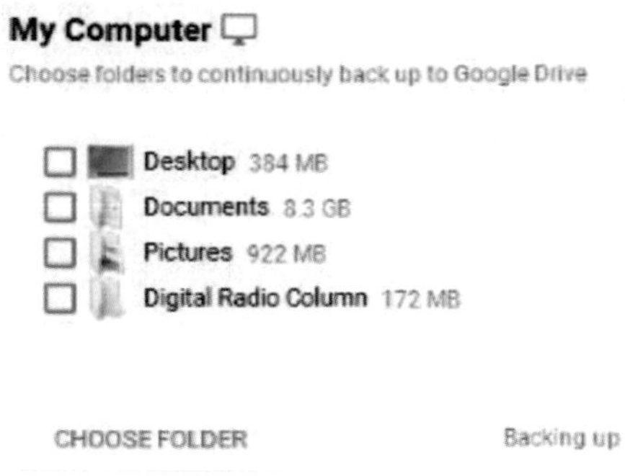

My Computer 🖵

Choose folders to continuously back up to Google Drive

☐ ▓ Desktop 384 MB
☐ ▓ Documents 8.3 GB
☐ ▓ Pictures 922 MB
☐ ▓ Digital Radio Column 172 MB

CHOOSE FOLDER   Backing up

Fig. 4.29 The best way is to clear any folder selections and then add using the CHOOSE FOLDER link.

Photo and video upload size Learn more

◯ High quality (free unlimited storage)
   Great visual quality at reduced file size

◉ Original quality (15.0 GB storage left)
   Full resolution that counts against your quota

Google Photos 🔖 Learn more

☐ Upload photos and videos to Google Photos
   Check your Photos settings to see which items Photos

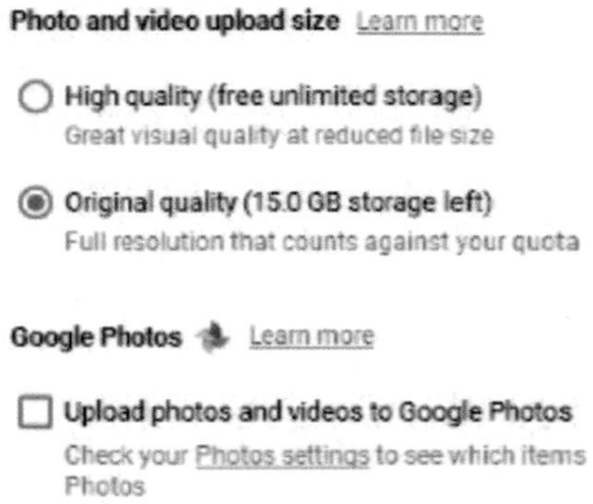

Fig. 4.30 Options for the handling of pictures.

If you need more space, you can upgrade for monthly charge, which gets you 100 GB of storage. If the folders you want to back up to My Drive (Figure 4.29) contain lots of images there are a couple of settings you should take a closer look at to make sure the tool works just the way you want it to (Figure 4.30).

The **Photo and video upload size ,** as the name suggests, lets you choose the upload size of videos and images. You can upload them in their original size or in what Google calls "High quality". If you take the first option, the images and videos you upload will count against your storage. The second option won't count against your storage quota. However, keep in mind that in this case photos and videos will be compressed to save space. You can also back up data from a smartphone, camera, SD card, or other devices. Just plug a phone or camera into your computer, click on the "USB devices & SD cards" at the bottom of the options list (Figure 4.31 on Page 50)and select the files you want to upload to the cloud from your connected device.

Removing Items

Once the relationship between your PC and My Drive is set up you can control the two-way backup process via preferences by accessing the Google Drive icon in the system tray on a PC.

Particularly important are what happens with deletion of files. There are three settings and the obvious one to choose is to **Ask me before removing items everywhere** as this is the safest option. There are options to globally delete a file or image using the option to **Remove Items Everywhere** and then to **Don't remove items everywhere** that will only delete the file or folder in the file system you are working on.

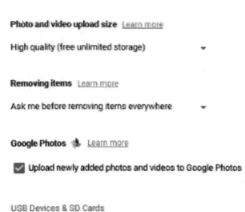

Fig. 4.31 You are able to upload directly from USB devices and SD cards

Viewing the files you have backed up to the cloud is easy. All you have to do is visit the My Drive website and click on the "Computers" tab on the left side. If you have backed up files from more than one computer, you'll see a different folder for each one.

Backup & Sync Google Photos

If you tick the box (Figure 4.31), images and videos located in the folders you selected in step two will automatically be uploaded to Google Photos. Unchecked, the images will only be uploaded to My Drive and won't show up in your Google Photos account. There's an option in Photo's <u>settings</u> that allows you to view your My Drive images and videos in your Photo's Library.

Google Calendar

The free calendar application can appear to have limited settings but it might just suit your needs. To add an event you just click on the day and when the diary page opens click on the time or click on More Options. Next you will see the options as shown in Figure 4.33 on page 52.

≡   **Goo**gle Calendar

May 2018   ‹ ›

S	M	T	W	T	F	S
29	30	1	2	3	4	5
6	7	8	9	10	11	12
13	14	15	16	17	18	19
20	21	22	23	24	25	26
27	28	29	30	31	1	2
3	4	5	6	7	8	9

Add a friend's calendar   +

My calendars   ⌃

☑ Kevin Ryan

☐ Reminders

Other calendars   ⌃

☐ Holidays in United Kingdom

Fig. 4.32 Google Calendar with my calendars and other calendars with civil information.

Now you can add in details like location , time and a map of the venue and choose whether you want to use Google Hangouts to connect people using video conferencing.

The editor is basic but has enough features to add the details your guests need to make their way to the meeting.

In the **Settings** you can change the time format, display multiple time zones and a world clock, set the default duration of meetings and have speedy meetings that finish early. Other settings let you add events from Gmail and automatically add video calls to events. There are alternative calendars for Chinese, Hebrew, Persian, Hirji, Korean and Indian. There are a host of other calendars in the **Browse calendars of interest** covering topics from religious holidays of various faiths to your favourite sports teams. The calendars have their own settings that you need to check.

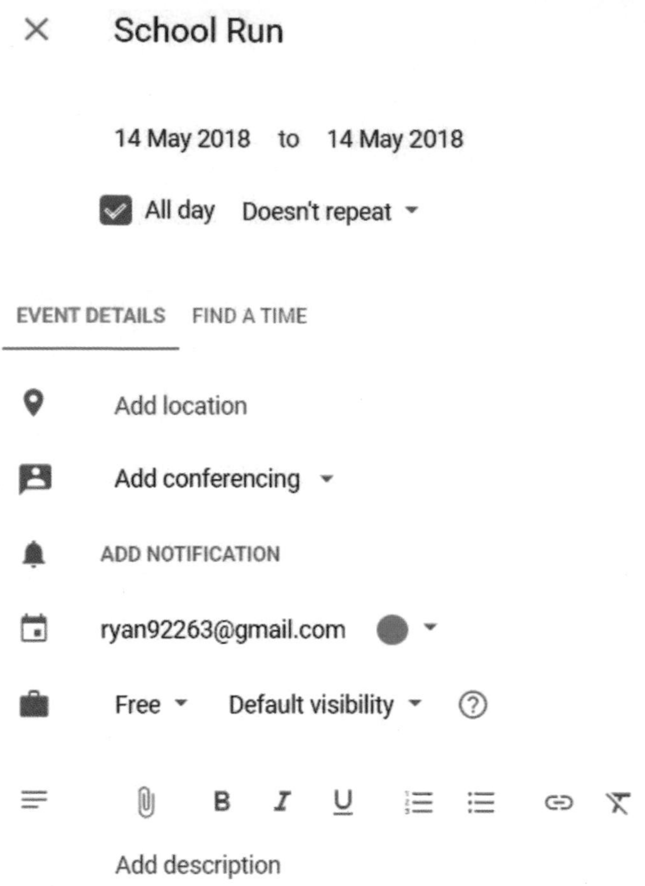

✕   **School Run**

14 May 2018   to   14 May 2018

☑ All day   Doesn't repeat ▾

EVENT DETAILS   FIND A TIME
_____

📍   Add location

🗨   Add conferencing ▾

🔔   ADD NOTIFICATION

📅   ryan92263@gmail.com   ⚫ ▾

💼   Free ▾   Default visibility ▾   ⑦

☰   📎   **B**   *I*   <u>U</u>   ☷   ☰   ⌗   ✗

Add description

Fig. 4.33 Once you add an event to a date you will find
that many other options become available.

It is possible to import calendar information from your PC but it
needs to be in either the iCal format or as a .CSV file. You need to
check if your current e-mail client will export the calendar in the
correct format and not all of them do. Finally, don't forget to Save
your calendar entry. The Save button is on the edge of the screen
and it is easy to forget to use it.

Using Calendar for Business

Google Calendar is a good personal product and might work in a small business once you understand its limitations. It does not have the features that a combination of Microsoft Exchange/ Outlook would provide. It works best when everyone is using it but it will send invitations to meetings using e-mail addresses outside of Gmail.

Google Contacts

Alongside Calendar is Google Contacts although it is not that well integrated with it. Adding a contact while scheduling a meeting puts the details in **Other Contacts** rather than **Contacts.** Adding contacts manually is easy and contacts can have multiple e-mail addresses that are filtered by **Labels.** There is a good guide in Contacts on using labels. Click on Create Label and give it a title. Then click on the label name you just created and a simple tutorial opens on how to implement them.

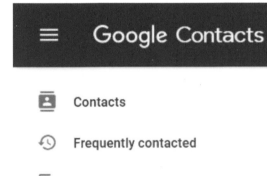

Fig. 4.34 Google Contacts is separate to Calendar rather than part of a general app like Microsoft Outlook.

In the transition between versions Google sometimes uses features in the old version until they have been implemented in the new one. I found this when Importing and exporting contacts using a .csv file. These functions hadn't been implemented yet in the **Preview Version** and Google switched me to the **Old Version.** The information transfers after you close and re-open the app.

Google Photos

Have old photos on your computer?

Install the new desktop uploader to safely back up photos from your computer and storage cards

NO, THANKS   GET THE UPLOADER

Fig. 4.35 Google will find and upload images and videos from your PC if you choose that option.

Google initially offers to store your old photos on Google Drive. The Uploader , Figure 4.35, is part of Google Backup and Sync. When you open Google Photos it will display all the images that you previously uploaded.

On the right hand side is a time slider , Figure 4.36, that sorts your images into the months they were uploaded.

You can also create your own **Albums** or use the preset ones to categorise your images. Using the **Assistant** you can **Share** your photos with another Google account, create a Movie or a **Collage**, **Clear the Clutter** by moving images to an **Archive** or use **Animation**.

Fig. 4.36 Part of the Google Photos dashboard showing the timeline slider that groups images by the month they were uploaded.

Blogger

As the name suggests Blogger is a tool to create your own blog. If you are happy being a subdomain on the well-known **blogspot.com** then it is easy to learn and use provided you stick to accepting most of the default settings.   Please heed the information on the use of cookies that now applies within the European Union.

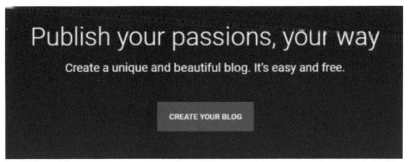

Fig. 4.37 The purpose of Blogger is clearly stated by Google.

Fig. 4.38 Create and style your blog using a pre-built theme . Change to a new theme whenever you wish.

Blogger has most of the features that you will need to create pages and posts. You find them on the menu on the dashboard.

· **Page**   DRM in India

Fig. 4.39 Just a part of the in-built editor that is feature rich.

The editor has plenty of features as shown in Figure 4.39 and there are options on how the published HTML will be displayed. The layout section lets you create menus, subscriptions and add other gadgets to various parts of the website.

Google Classroom

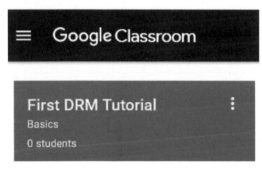

If you work in a school or other educational establishment then there are restrictions on using this product. Check the restrictions before investing a lot of time in creating your lessons.

Fig. 4.40 Classroom is easy to learn and use.

Through this product you can create all sorts of material to help customers understand your products and services or activities in your club or organisation where some element of self learning is involved.

It is simple to learn but the thing that might trip you up is security as Google will only invite students from a trusted domain. Defining just what Google sees as a trusted domain is difficult to pin down and you might need help from Google to make it work.

Cross Device Working

The Google office apps are both extensions in Google Chrome for Windows and available as separate apps. On iOS (Figure 4.41) and Android there are separate apps for Docs, Sheets and Slides available on the respective app stores.

Fig. 4.41 Google apps on iOS11.

Browser Compatibility

Google Docs, Sheets and Slides works on Chrome, Firefox and Microsoft's Internet Explorer and Edge browser although the latter three do not support offline working. The best option is to use Google Chrome.

Google Docs Summary

Google Docs will be adequate for many people with 15GB of free storage and an office suite that keep improving. A free Google account also includes the messaging app called Hangouts, Google Translate and the geographic apps Google Earth and Maps.

If you are starting out with your own business or are self employed then Google Docs includes nearly everything you need to interact with your customers. You can create a simple website using Blogger and contact clients using Gmail and Hangouts.

As your business grows I think you will want to upgrade from Google Docs to have a business name that is included in your email address and in the name of your website. You can add these on the side of Google Docs but when you want business information to flow automatically then you need to consider using Google's G Suite or Microsoft Office 365.

5

Google G Suite

G Suite by Google Cloud

Fig. 5.1 G Suite is Google Docs for Business or Professional users.

GSuite is a package of cloud computing services that is aimed at business and education. It has three levels **Basic**, **Business** and **Enterprise**. There is **GSuite for Education** that provides the Business edition free of change to qualifying institutions and Google requires interested schools to formally apply for it.

GSuite for Non Profit Organisations is available in the UK provided they are registered with tt-exchange and must have recognizable charitable status. The application takes some time to complete and organisations have to upload relevant documentation. There is comprehensive information at **https:// www. tt-exchange.org/google-for-non-profits_faqs**.

As the name suggests the **Enterprise** version is for big business with tens or hundreds of users. **GSuite for Government** is only available in the USA.

Do I need G Suite?

This is a good question and depends on your experience to date and what you need to achieve. If you are new to working with office suite of applications online then I would suggest starting with Google Docs to see if you are comfortable with the concept and with the basic operations of the three main apps.

The apps are functionally the same in both versions but G Suite has the business orientated features enabled. These centre around sharing and co-authoring documents in ways that are not possible in Google Docs and around managing other users that are part of your G Suite account.

The second question is what do you really get by paying a monthly fee per user? Charts comparing the two products can list up to fifty functions that are not available in Docs but they may not matter to you.

The Basic level in GSuite looks similar to the freely available Google Docs apart from the increased amount of online storage. GSuite is a business tool and from the start it is set up with an administrator that manages and controls what other users can do. GSuite has many security levels and real-time collaboration between users on documents meaning they can work together rather than waiting for one member of the team to save their changes. GSuite is very security conscious and is strengthening its anti-hacker defences on a regular basis.

The product is supported by Google technical staff, has training resources available and has a guaranteed up-time even if that is just 99.9%.

Legal	Auditing and archiving built in.
Calendars	Individual, team and event calendars.
Video	Uses Hangouts Meet.
Users	Multiple user accounts and user access controls.
Collaboration	Synchronous editing, multiple projects, real time updating.
Geographical Maps	Add them to your documents.

Fig. 5.2 Some of the features found in in the apps in G Suite but not in Google Docs version.

Google Docs is a personal product without any support and collaboration is by exchanging documents between users.

Both Google products work on most devices and are compatible with files created in other programs, such as Microsoft Office.

Advantages of G Suite

GSuite ensures all the apps work as a suite of products whereas in Google Docs they are the same apps but they are configured to work in a standalone way. For instance, in G Suite you can receive a message in Gmail and instantly convert it into a Calendar event. When you make a comment in Docs, Sheets or Slides, collaborators automatically receive email alerts.

With G Suite, you get a number of additional business-grade services which are not included with Google's free consumer apps. These services include 24/7 phone and email support, custom business email *name@yourcompany.co.uk*, twice the amount of cloud storage across **Gmail** and **Drive**, 99.9% guaranteed uptime on business email, interoperability with Microsoft Outlook, additional security options such as two-step authentication and Single Sign On (SSO), and administrative controls for user accounts.

Technical Knowledge

GSuite is aimed at business users and depending on how much you have invested in your web presence it may be more demanding to set up than you expect in terms of the time you have to devote to learning about the administration of the system.

G Suite has to be connected to a domain that you own and Google pushes you strongly through frequent reminders during the setup phase to move your e-mail accounts onto Gmail. There is more detailed information on making this move in Appendix 3 that should help you decide if you want to make the change. I have moved e-mail handling from the hosting company that originally handled my e-mails and it does work.

Your Options

Figure 5.3 lists some typical starting points for users or businesses moving to G Suite and my recommended solution. Use these as a guide and not as definitive solutions. G Suite and Google Docs are separate systems and data or folder sharing won't transfer between them as part of an upgrade.

Your Current Position	Suggested Course of Action
Established web presence and e-mail but unsure about the technical stuff.	Attach your domain to G Suite but keep your e-mail accounts as they are. This won't affect your website and email messages continue to be handled by your current provider.
Established web presence, and good technically.	If you can accept the outage of e-mail for a short period complete the whole transfer process.
Established web presence that you don't want to change and have good technical skills.	Set up a new domain and use that for G Suite setup and management including e-mails. E-Mail aliases and other tricks may be needed to make everything work seamlessly.
Have a website that is not critical for my activities.	Use that domain name and let Google do the whole process from start to finish.
Starting out.	Let Google do the whole process from start to finish including creating your domain name.

Fig. 5.3 A few scenarios with suggested courses of action.

Domain Name

Attaching a domain is not a big problem and it does not affect any websites that use that domain name. For example, I started a G Suite trial using my **.kpr-web.co.uk** domain and that did not affect my business website **www.kpr-web.co.uk.**

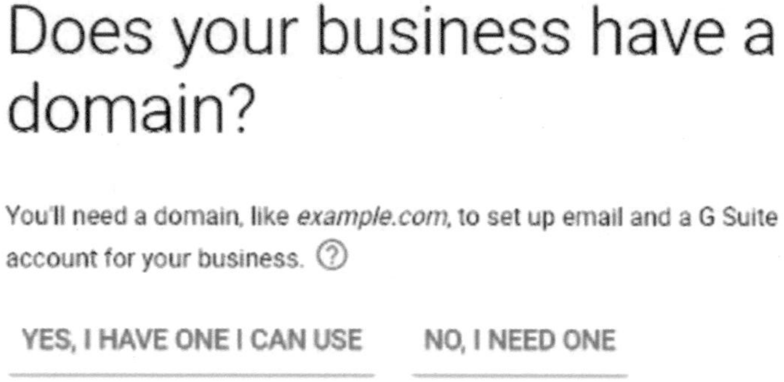

Does your business have a domain?

You'll need a domain, like *example.com*, to set up email and a G Suite account for your business. ⓘ

YES, I HAVE ONE I CAN USE   NO, I NEED ONE

Fig. 5.4 The opening question from GSuite concerns any existing domain names that you plan to use.

Figure 5.4 is the first question in the G Suite setup procedure and there are more questions around using an existing domain owned by you or your business including opting to buy a new domain through Google. Buying a new domain will overcome any possible security issues that Google might detect with an existing domain. I have had Google raise security issues on domains that I have from trusted hosting companies without much explanation as to how I might fix the problem.

To proceed with the setup you ideally need to understand basic internet concepts such as domains and sub-domains and DNS records and possibly FTP to transfer files from your device to web folders. Have any account details provided by your hosting company on how to login to your hosting packages configuration portal to hand, in case you need to fall back on their support teams if you are unsure about anything.

Email Accounts

You may know that Web sites' names and their corresponding technical internet addresses (an IPv4 address of the form 34.78.245.56) are stored in an online directory called the DNS or Domain Name System.

You may not know that e-mail servers have entries in the same directory. A mail exchanger **record** (**MX record**) is a type of verified **record** in the Domain Name System that specifies a mail server responsible for accepting email messages on behalf of a recipient's domain, and a preference value used to prioritize mail delivery if multiple mail servers are available.

G Suite asks you to add MX records that give its servers priority of those on your hosting account. G Suite has guides for many of the well known hosting companies but it is not an exhaustive list and there is a bias to US companies.

To implement the transfer you may need to access your hosting setup using CPanel or Plesk. Your hosting company will have provided you details on how to do this. They will resend them if you can't find your copy. You have to accept that you or your business may be without reliable e-mail for up to 48 hours. You can crash out of the setup process and not do this. There does not seem to be an elegant way of doing this.

Trying G Suite

Google lets prospective users try their three editions for free but I recommend starting with the **Basic** edition as there is more than enough to learn at this entry level. The URL is **https://gsuite.google.com/signup** and Google does not ask for any financial commitment at this stage.

It is not made clear up-front but G Suite's aim is to integrate some of your business resources with its own platforms. For example, it doesn't want to host your website but tries to move your e-mail over to Gmail.

G Suite Business Account

Not all the steps are covered in the next few pages that aim to show you the level of knowledge required to set up and administer G Suite. You may have to go back a step now and again to change some information and that is OK. G Suite needs an administrator , Figure 5.5, and you will need to provide a user ID and password and business e-mail. You also need a secondary e-mail address on a different domain for security and recovery. Finally you need to agree to the Terms and Conditions.

What's your name?

You'll be the G Suite account admin since you're creating the account. Don't worry, you can assign this role to someone else later.

Fig 5.5 G Suite needs an administrator to manage users and other resources. You can give this job to someone else or create additional administrators.

Change Domains

If you think that you made a mistake in linking your current business domain then you will want to untangle it. You have some options here. You can cancel your subscription. Once you click on the **cancel subscription link** the warnings messages seem to indicate that you are going to wipe everything you have in Google. They are designed to make you stop and think. If you have just tried out G Suite then you can cancel your subscription without any concerns. To be safe I recommend contacting G Suite support who will check the status of your account and configuration and advise you on the best course of action.

Adding a Domain

Happily, G Suite will work with multiple domains because they know that businesses have several domains and also acquire and merge with other businesses.

When you set up G Suite you use a primary domain. You can change this especially if you no longer own this domain or you are re-inventing your business an need a different domain name. The process is too detailed to cover here but there is a lot of help information at **https://support.google.com**.

Other domains can be added as secondary domains or sub-domains that is useful for giving two or more teams a common identity while keeping the ownership and brand of the individual domains. Again there is a lot of detail in the Google support pages.

Setting Up G Suite

Now is the time to add users (Figure 5.6) to your business account and you do this as the account administrator.

Set up a business account
You'll be able to manage G Suite for your entire team.

Add people to your G Suite account
Create user accounts for everyone on your team so they can sign in to their new business Gmail, Drive, Calendar, and more.

Verify your domain and set up email
Verify that you own your domain and set up email for your business.

Fig. 5.6 Add people as users to your Business Account.

The administrator can login to the admin console and use the G Suite apps but consider treating the administrator as a separate entity that only uses the Admin Console. The main reason is that the administrator has top level permissions and that person should login occasionally as an ordinary user to make sure they are setting other users up correctly.

Verify Your Domain

Google requires verification that you own the domain that it is being linked to. Google's preferred method is that you edit the HTML code on the home page of your website although there are other methods available (Figure 5.7). My own preference is to upload a small file to the root directory on the website either via an FTP client or through the File Manager in the website's control panel. Google offers plenty of help on this but assumes that you know what it is talking about and you may not!

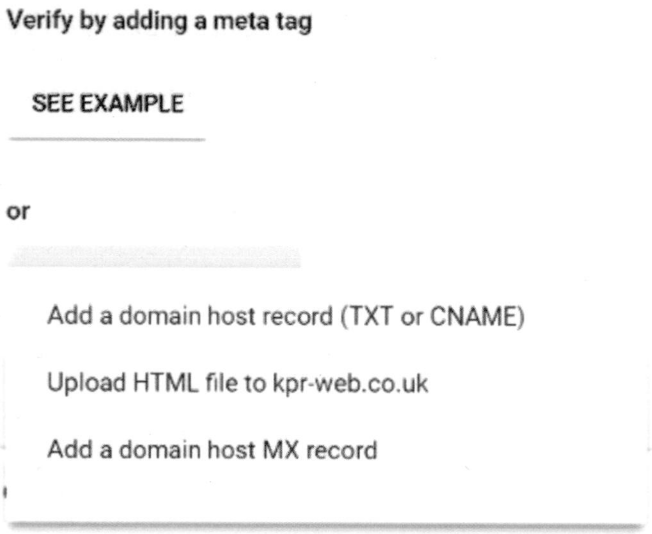

Verify by adding a meta tag

SEE EXAMPLE

or

Add a domain host record (TXT or CNAME)

Upload HTML file to kpr-web.co.uk

Add a domain host MX record

Fig. 5.7 Google has four options, and the least complex is uploading HTML file to the domain root using FTP or via your hosting package's configuration panel.

Setting Up Email

The final step is setting up, and by this G Suite means transferring the e-mail infrastructure from your existing hosting company to Gmail by deleting the existing MX (**M**ail e**X**change) records that tell other internet users where the mailboxes are and inserting new MX records to point other mail delivery systems to Gmail. This is done all the time and should be pain-free but if you are running a trial I recommend opting out no matter how many times G Suite prompts you do proceed with the transfer.

There is no clearly labelled option to skip the e-mail steps so I opted for a **Manual Setup** and then ticked the box (Figure 5.8) that all users had been set up.

Kevin Ryan (You)
kevin1@kpr-web.co.uk

 I added all user email addresses currently using **@kpr-web.co.uk**.

Fig. 5.8 Bypass the e-mail transfer by telling G Suite that it is done.

Whenever you open the G Suite Admin Console there will be a reminder at the top that e-mail step has not been completed and that billing is also outstanding.

Using Gmail

Moving your e-mail handling from an existing host to Gmail is a technical process and I have put a short guide in Appendix 3. Once signed up to GSuite you can check all aspects of e-mail including security features by logging in to your GSuite administrator's account and following the menu path of **Apps -> G Suite -> Settings for Gmail**.

After setup Gmail will have welcome e-mails in each new user's inbox that have not been downloaded to your mail client. I tend to leave them in the Gmail inbox so when they download you know that your e-mail handling has swapped over to Google.

G Suite Basic   Active

Users: 3

Payment plan	Flexible Plan
Users	3
Currency	GBP
Cost	£3.30 per user per month
Est. monthly bill	£9.90 per month
Contract expires	No contract

Fig. 5.9 Basic information about my kpr-cloud.co.uk plan. There is a separate Actions menu to configure the payment method and cancel the subscription.

Billing

At some stage of the setup process you will be asked by Google to set up billing using either a credit card or direct debit on your bank account. The reminder happens randomly and it can vary between the very start and the very end of the process, and you can proceed with the trial if you like.

Remember you only get a 14-day trial period and that really isn't long enough to get familiar with G Suite. You can revisit billing by clicking on the Billing icon in G Suite's dashboard and you may want to get a subscription that is on a rolling monthly basis as shown in Figure 5.9.

G Suite isn't that expensive and it is worth investing in the extra time to explore the collaboration and sharing features as well gaining experience in setting up user accounts and getting them to work on another PC or tablet device.

Billing Information

Transactions

May 1 – 14, 2018	£4.15
Apr 1 – 30, 2018	£9.90
Mar 1 – 31, 2018	£1.59

Fig 5.10 April is a full month for three users at £3.30 each. Part months are hard to work out.

As shown in Figure 5.10 , G Suite provides detailed information on your bills including downloads if you need them.

The billing is listed per month even if you only used G Suite for a few days.

It is a pay-per-use system that is charged per day but I find it hard to work out their daily/weekly rates if you start part way through a billing cycle.

Create a new user

Bill	Williams
bill	@kpr-cloud.co.uk

Temporary password will be assigned - **Set Password**

ADDITIONAL INFO

Fig. 5.11 User information and Additional Info lets you add more details such as telephone numbers.

Adding Users

Adding new users is easy to do provided you do so in a logical manner. If you are working on a single device both as the account admin and then as the user you just created you must be disciplined and log off from all instances of your administrator accounts. It is easy to forget to do this and you can get very baffling results.

Bill Williams   Never logged in   0 GB

Fig. 5.12 Check the status of a user and take action if you their entry is clearly incorrect.

This happens because G Suite detects any unexplained activity and create accounts that are both suspended and able to work (Figure 5.12). If you get any sort of anomaly then the only solution is to delete and recreate that account. It is far better to use one device for admin and another to test that users can login and that you have given them the apps they need to do their jobs. Once everything is set up click on Send Email to forward the setup information to that user at their current e-mail address. In the Admin Console's User area you can resend that information, delete or suspend the user.

Set Up Your Company Structure

Name	Description
▾ kpr-cloud.co.uk	kpr-cloud.co.uk
IT Support	IT and database team
Sales	Web team

Fig. 5.13 A simple company structure with two teams ready for you to add users.

The users are listed in the **Directory** section of the Admin Console. You put users into groups or organizational units (OUs) as shown in Figure 5.13. Groups is a useful feature if you work with many people or need to create project teams. Use OUs to deploy different G Suite apps .

Reports

G Suite has many reports that keep track of just about everything.

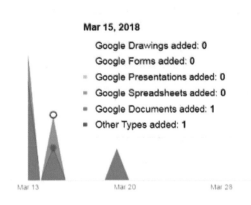

Mar 15, 2018

Google Drawings added: 0
Google Forms added: 0
Google Presentations added: 0
Google Spreadsheets added: 0
Google Documents added: 1
Other Types added: 1

Mar 13   Mar 20   Mar 28

Fig. 5.14 Detailed statistics are available in a dashboard and as more detailed information by drilling down via hotspots.

Check the number of licences in use, available storage, apps usage including over usage of apps that detract from work. The dashboard provides a good overview of the available statistics and hovering over each area expands the data underlying the graphic as shown in Figure 5.14. Alerts are available to notify the administrator of any suspicious activity and changes to user accounts.

G Suite Admin

Admin roles

CREATE A NEW ROLE

System Roles ❓

Super Admin

Groups Admin

User Management Admin

Help Desk Admin

Services Admin

Mobile Admin

Fig. 5.15 Spread the load by creating other admins to look after Groups, etc.

You won't be able to manage G Suite by just signing in as the administrator and playing with it. Like all back-end systems it is not always logical in how it does things or on where you find a particular configuration setting. The administrator functions are listed in Appendix 2.

You don't have to do all this by yourself and you can create other administrators to look after some of the tasks (Figure 5.15). The areas that usually take up a lot of time are User Management Admin and Mobile Admin because problems are so varied.

Your main problems will be with user management and trying to resolve anomalies with their status. Google is quick to suspend users and it can be difficult to change a status other than by deleting and recreating them.

The other area that can be particularly troublesome is with the security of your G Suite account where you want to accommodate domains outside the very secure Google environment. Make full use of the Google Support team.

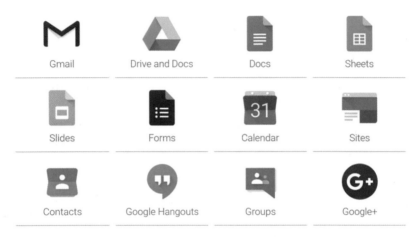

Fig. 5.16 Users see the range of apps available to them when they login to G Suite.

G Suite Apps

As the G Suite administrator you can send setup instructions to users using an e-mail address that is not part of your new G Suite account. Users have to respond to it to enable their access to the account you created.

They can then login to G Suite where they are presented with the screen shown in Figure 5.16. Clicking on each icon will open a new tab in your browser where you need to complete a few more setup tasks for each application.

Online Training

G Suite Learning Center

Fig. 5.17 G Suite has many learning resources to help you.

The first thing to do is to take the short tour of the Admin console that shows you where some of the controls are. Google has online training (Figure 5.17) including a Quick Start Guide to get you up and running in 7 steps. It is split in these entry points.

Learn By Product— This section provides a guide, a two-page cheat sheet for reference, tips , frequently asked questions and moving from Microsoft.

Tips Library is a blog of featured tips, tips sorted by product and tips under a few broad headings.

Moving from Microsoft starts with collaborating with non G Suite users and has sections on moving email, calendars, documents, spreadsheets, presentations and video calls from the equivalent Microsoft applications

Use at Work — this section is split into learning by industry, learning by typical roles and learning by task.

Collaborative Working (Sharing)

Once you have two users set up you can check how fast collaborative working displays any changes. The document has to be **shared** and those two users can make changes and chat to each other online about what they are doing.   Ideally you should carry out the testing using two different devices. If the two users open the document at the same time they see the changes the other is making as they make them. Both need to be in editing mode.

Fig. 5.18 The Share button in an app lets you share the document and check who has access to it.

This is the big difference between G Suite and Google Docs.

In the latter you can share documents and they appear on your recipient's list of available documents. The editing permissions are those you have given the document. Changes are applied to the document at the end of the editing process. In Google G Suite (Figure 5.18) The document is also shared with certain permissions and changes are applied almost in real time to each copy of the document.

Google Vault

Google Vault is available only in one of the Enterprise plans. It is a document management system and a store that can be used for several purposes. The first is **Archiving** documents for legal or historical reasons and administrators set retention rules to control how long data is retained before being removed from user accounts and deleted from Google systems. Time scales are set in days and data can be stored indefinitely (Figure 5.19).

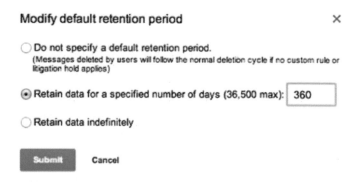

Fig. 5.19 Google Vault has three settings to control data retention, a critical factor for many companies.

The Search function indexes your domain's data by user account, organizational unit, date, or keyword. Linked to Search is **Export** that lets you download your search results although Google limits how long a search is allowed to run. The administrator can generate **Audit reports** to learn about actions Vault users have taken during a specified period of time. Vault is part of the Business & Enterprise editions.

Google Cloud Search

Another tool in the Business and Enterprise editions. Like the

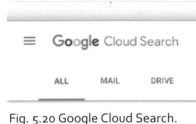

Fig. 5.20 Google Cloud Search.

Search function in Google Vault, Cloud Search harnesses the power of the Google search engine to search documents, emails, events and any corporate directories for the information you want (Figure 5.20). If you like the idea of a digital assistant that works with your company data then you need to upgrade to the Business Edition that is twice the price per user of the Basic Edition. However the plan gives you unlimited storage if you have more than five users and 1TB per user below that limit.

G Suite Summary

In this chapter you learned how G Suite works and about the skills you should have or need to acquire through exploring its training videos. The main apps in G Suite are the same as in Google Docs with enhanced sharing features.

G Suite is a multi-user system but individuals and sole traders gain increased storage, other business apps such as video conferencing and support for a modest amount each month. The issue you may have is one of finding the time to set up G Suite either through teaching your self or working with Google support.

6
Microsoft Office Online

Microsoft's range of products for personal and business are very similar to those offered by Google with an almost a one-for-one equivalent for each app.

| Account | Outlook | Office | Skype | OneDrive |
| Xbox Live | Bing | Store | Windows | MSN |

Fig. 6.1 Microsoft states that all these service are free with an online account but not all of them are strictly a cloud computing service.

Microsoft's Office Online is a suite of apps bundled in with OneDrive. Online storage provider Box also uses Office Online to open documents stored in its system.

Getting Started with Microsoft

Before using any online services you must have or obtain a Microsoft Account that only takes a short while to set up. I have two accounts and if you are an existing Microsoft customer and just looking at possibilities then consider setting up a second account.

The process is easy and logical and you should add in one of the suggested forms of authentication. I usually opt for two-stage authentication to a mobile telephone where you receive a text message with a single use PIN number to validate your login.

Sign in

Email, phone or Skype

Next

No account? Create one!

Fig. 6.2 The Microsoft page for existing and new accounts.

Point your browser at **https://login.live.com** and follow the link to create an account as shown in Figure 6.2 or to log in using your existing account.

OneDrive

OneDrive sits at the heart of Microsoft's cloud computing services. The free plan provides you with 5GB of storage. You can access OneDrive through a browser but it also has a desktop app for Windows with useful features. The download link for the software is located at this URL, **https://onedrive.live.com/about/en-GB/download,** where all you need to do is choose your Windows operating system. OneDrive is bundled with Windows 10 and don't need to download the software a second time.

After you download the application and install it, a OneDrive folder appears on your Windows device that you store files in like any other Windows folder. OneDrive can be an extension to your local storage, an online backup repository or hold a shadow copy of important files on your Windows device. Once it is installed an icon, two white or blue clouds together, is added to your system tray at the bottom right of your Windows desktop.

File Sync with OneDrive

One of the tasks you can use OneDrive for is to create a backup of important documents and projects that are updated as you make changes. In this regard, it is important to understand the limitations of the personal version of OneDrive.

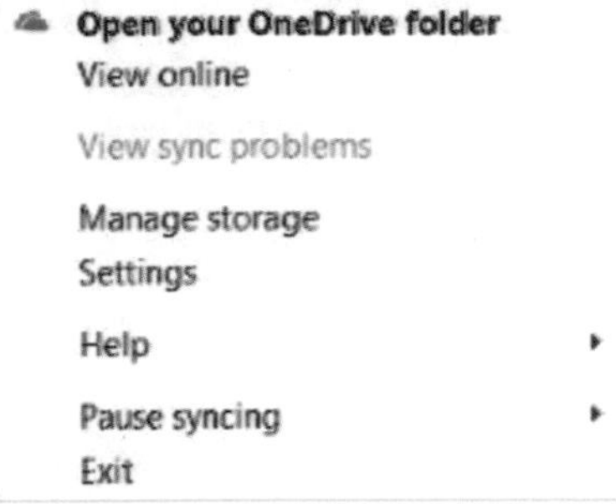

⬆ **Open your OneDrive folder**
View online

View sync problems

Manage storage

Settings

Help   ▸

Pause syncing   ▸
Exit

Fig. 6.3 Access the file sync menu using Settings.

Right click on the OneDrive icon in the system tray and open the **Settings** menu (Figure 6.3) to set up **file synchronization** often abbreviated to **file sync**. You might think that you sync files to OneDrive but it is designed to work the other way round. Folders and Files created on OneDrive are copied back to the local device to allow users to work offline.

To set up a link between the local and online copies you need to move files and folders from your local device to OneDrive and then sync them back to the OneDrive folder on your PC. This concept does seem a bit back to front. Unfortunately, this is Microsoft's new policy of moving everything possible to the cloud. It is easy once you complete the process a few times.

Windows Backup and Restore application won't use the free version of OneDrive, it will work if you have a paid-for subscription, as it doesn't include OneDrive in its available options. You have to use a third party product that supports OneDrive as a backup destination. However, don't forget that 5GB is a generous but not a huge amount of storage space and even simple backups can use this up very quickly.

Compare this with Google Drive that works the same as OneDrive in terms of synchronising files from the cloud to your PC but also has the reverse feature of synchronising from the PC to Google Drive. Google Drive provides three times the storage of OneDrive.

Working in OneDrive

Fig. 6.4 The Office Online button in Chrome expands to show the six main Web Apps and a list of Recent Documents.

The free version of OneDrive is a powerful tool that gives you access to **Word Online, Excel Online** and **PowerPoint Online**. These versions are available both on free and paid-for OneDrive plans and are different to the full blown Office 365 and Office 2016 standalone versions.

You use these versions when you open files stored on OneDrive using a web browser. As shown in Fig. 6.4 you also get access to **Outlook** and **OneNote**.

There are a couple of ways to use the Microsoft Office applications to access your files in OneDrive.

The first and simplest way is to login into OneDrive and then open an application and then load the corresponding file or choose a file and then click to open it.

OneDrive on Android and iOS

OneDrive is available for both these operating systems and works well on versions 9-11 of iOS and versions 4-7 of Android. Both systems have versions of Word, Excel and PowerPoint apps available in their respective stores to download to your desktop.

The apps let you open files in OneDrive, other cloud storage services and on your device. The list that opens when you click on **Add a place** includes OneDrive Personal and OneDrive for Business and any other installed providers in addition to any apps already installed on your device. The list shown for Android is short in comparison to the longer list of cloud storage providers that have an iOS app.

Browser Compatibility

Microsoft has guidelines on which browsers will work with Office Online. On **Windows** 7 (SP1), 8. 8.1 and 10 , Internet Explorer 11, Firefox and Chrome should work without any issues. Windows 10 also supports the Edge browser. If you are still using Windows Vista then it must be at the SP2 level. Firefox and Chrome will work but some features may not be available.

On **Apple**, Safari and Chrome will work on Mac OS X (10.8) or later. On the iPad and iPhone the recommendation is to use the Office apps. Safari may work on older versions of the Operating System (OS).

Android users should use the Office for Android apps on all versions as no Android browsers are officially supported.

The list will change over time and if you experience any problems with your browser check the Microsoft support pages for their most up to date recommendations.

Chrome Web Apps

Fig. 6.5 The orange icon opens the Microsoft Web Apps.

On Windows 7 there is an **Office Online Extension** for Chrome that you **Add to Chrome** and it places an icon to the Chrome System Tray as shown in Figure 6.5.

Clicking on the square orange button opens a menu box (please refer to Figure 6.4 on page 80) listing the six main Web Apps and a list of Recent Documents that were added to OneDrive.

There is a button to **Upload and Open** documents from your local device. The appropriate app will open depending on the type of file selected for upload. Of course, if the file is in a format that is not supported on OneDrive you will see an error message. If you open any of three Office Web Apps you will see an option to upload files.

Upload a Word Document and the contents will be displayed like a file ready for printing. There is no editing toolbar but there is a button to **Edit Document**.

The Office Online Web Apps use the latest formats and if the file is in an older format you will see a warning message that a copy of the document will be made in the latest format if you opt to **Convert** it or that your local copy of Word will open if you want to retain the old format.

Firefox Web Apps

On Windows 7 there is an **Add-On for Firefox** labelled **Office Online** that gives access to both Office Online and Google Services. Firefox provides links to all the apps in OneDrive as shown in Figure 6.6. You see the same set of apps using the OneDrive menu bar.

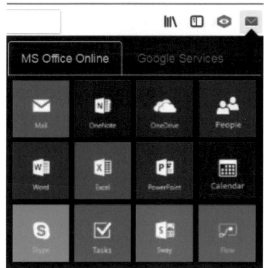

Once you sign-in to your account you get the same user experience as in Chrome.

On Windows 10 you may fall foul of security that will prevent you adding the extension.

Fig. 6.6 Firefox can provide access to two major providers on a single button.

Internet Explorer and Edge

OneDrive works with IE but you have to login manually to your OneDrive account. The URL is **https://onedrive.live.com** where you will see the menu shown in Figure 6.7. The default location is **Files** and **Photos** are filtered into a separate list. PCs lists all the devices that have OneDrive installed but don't be surprised if you can't access the OneDrive folder on a particular device.

OneDrive

Files

Recent

Photos

Shared

Recycle bin

PCs

File Formats

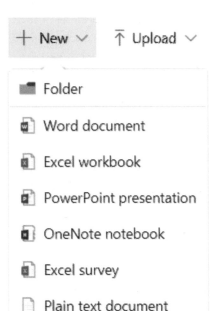

Fig. 6.7 OneDrive opens its default location of Files.

OneDrive and by extension Office Online supports file creation using a number of common Microsoft formats as shown in Fig. 6.8. Word, Excel and PowerPoint will work with documents in other formats but will convert it to docx, .xlsx or .pptx respectively and open that copy.

Word Online

Word Online has fewer functions than other versions but you can still create great documents. The first limitation is the number of **templates** available, recently reduced to nine and without access to Office.com for more.

Fig. 6.8 The New button lists the file formats that you can create documents in. OneDrive will open other formats.

Fig. 6.9 Word Online on a mobile Windows device.

You can't add your own templates or **text styles**. There are no options to change how the document will **print.** Word Online displays the print view at all times although it has an option to create a **Printable PDF.**

There is a built-in **spellchecker** but no option to add words to the **dictionary**. For somebody like me who writes technical articles this is a big drawback. The simplicity has its positive side. I find that **Tables** are much easier to create and style because the tool bar and right-click menus are less complex with fewer options.

Word Online will open most PDF documents for viewing but will also convert them so that they can be edited in Word Online. It means you can extract data from a PDF for a community website or a newsletter.

Word on Windows Mobile

On smaller screens, like mobile phones the number of visible menus are cut down and using it is for an extended period of time is not a great experience. The menu options are all there (Figure 6.9) but they are either sub-menu items collected under drop-down or scrolling menus. In landscape mode (the app is slightly more usable than in portrait mode. The point is that once your documents are stored on OneDrive they are accessible by a wide variety of devices using different operating systems. They are also very secure as they are backed up across the Microsoft network.

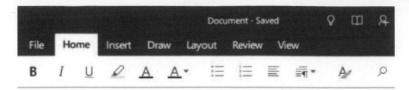

Fig. 6.10 Word menu on a 10 inch screen using Android in portrait mode which has a reduced visible menu.

Fig. 6.11 Word Online as opened on a Windows 7 desktop in a more familiar format .

Word on Android and iOS

A small part of the main screen for the Word app running on Android 7 is shown in Figure 6.10. The **Home** menu is reduced to the **Fonts**, missing out the Paragraph and **Styles** menu items. Compare this to Word Online when opened on a desktop (Figure 6.11). The apps present differently on iOS and Android and also between landscape and portrait modes.

Excel Online

Excel Online works using the latest format which is .xlsx and any workbooks on OneDrive in the Excel 97-2003 (.xls format), binary workbook file (.xlsb), OpenDocument Spreadsheet (.ods) will be converted to .xlsx. Excel macro-enabled workbooks (.xlsm) will also be converted but the macros do not run in Excel Online. Files in the .csv format are not supported.

In general, calculations, charts and tables, pivot tables and charts and dates work exactly the same as Excel 2016. If you use data connections then it is worth checking to see if Excel Online supports them.

Fig. 6.12 Excel online is almost as powerful as Excel installed on a desktop.

The differences, and they are understandable in an environment like OneDrive, are in very advanced features such as ActiveX controls, data validation,   rights management and digital signatures. Operations on cell data are all available in the online version of Excel (Figure 6.12). Fonts are generally the same in style and size but Excel Online might replace a very specific font that is not in common use with a standard one.

Very importantly, workbooks that are encrypted with password protection cannot be viewed in Excel Online. You can protect a worksheet, part of a workbook, and it can still be viewed by Excel Online. Protection can only be changed via desktop Excel. Most functions (Fig. 6.13) are the same in both versions of Excel and only a few now behave differently.

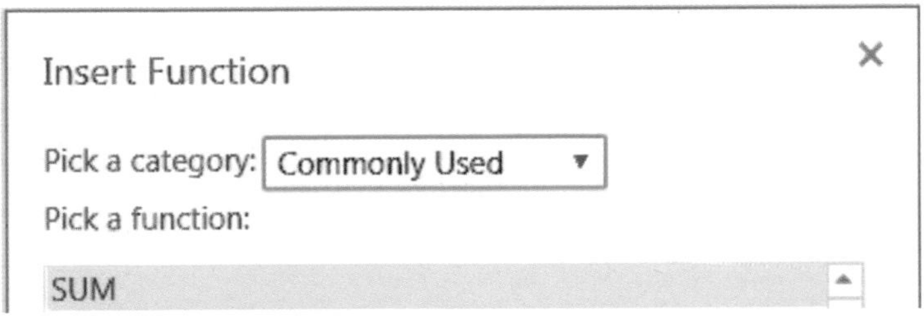

Insert Function   ✕

Pick a category: | Commonly Used   ▾ |
Pick a function:

SUM   ▴

Fig. 6.13 You will find all the familiar functions in Excel Online.

Excel Online saves your work automatically each time you make a change and you can download a copy to work on locally either in .xls or .ods format.

PowerPoint Online

Compared to Word and Excel, PowerPoint Online is very different to the desktop version as shown in Figure 6.14.

Desktop PowerPoint	PowerPoint Online
Print Menu has options for full page slides, notes page,	Only prints one slide per page
View Menu has Normal, Outline, Master and Reading	Editing view the only option.
Presenter View	Not yet available
Speaker Notes	Available put they can't be
Media Files	Restrictions on the size of
Slide Show View	Added in 2018.
Find and Replace	You can find text but you can't replace it.
Themes	Limited gallery available online.

Fig. 6.14 A comparison of the two versions. The Online version is slowly getting more functionality.

Office Online on iOS

The way Microsoft Office Online works on iOS depends on which version of iOS you are running. After the introduction of iOS 10 Microsoft decided not to update some of its apps in the Apple store. On iOS 9 you may be offered the option to download an older version of the app, as shown in Figure 6.15 but not for everyone and these will probably be withdrawn shortly.

Fig. 6.15 A previous version of iOS may let you get and install a compatible older version on your device.

iOS 9

On iOS 9 I was able to download older versions of Word, Excel, PowerPoint and OneDrive. The OneNote app now requires iOS 10 or later. Versions of Office Lens, a scanning app and Microsoft Edge were also available. The Apple store lists all the available apps and you only find out their compatibility status by getting and installing them.

iOS 10/iOS 11

These versions of iOS support the full range of Microsoft apps in the Apple Store. The main Microsoft Office apps are almost identical in layout to the older versions in IOS 9 but there are subtle differences because of recent updates to new versions.

Word Online on iOS

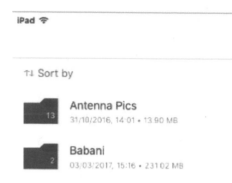

Fig. 6.16 OneDrive as opened on iOS 9.

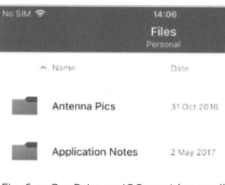

Fig. 6.17 OneDrive on iOS 11 with a small makeover for file and folder sorting.

Login to your OneDrive account as shown in Figure 6.16 for iOS 9 and in Figure 6.17 for iOS 11. iOS 9 lists the contents of OneDrive in a single column with name, date and size while iOS 11 has two columns with just name and date.

Tap on a file to select it and the suggested app will be shown in the top menu bar , Figure 6.18. Tap on this icon to launch Word Online to edit your document.

The Word app hasn't changed a lot in functionality. The latest iOS11 version (V2.13) handles more image formats and has had a number of bug fixes applied to it.

Fig. 6.18 Word Online on iOS 9 is shown as the recommended app to open Word and PDF files.

App	iOS 9	App	iOS 9
Word	☑	To-do	☑
Excel	☑	Planner	☒
PowerPoint	☑	Power BI	☒
OneNote	☒	Visio Viewer	☒
Outlook	☒	Sway	☒
Translator	☒	Authenticator	☑
SharePoint	☒	Yammer	☒
Teams	☒	Dynamics	☑

Fig. 6.19 Microsoft has not maintained backward compatibility with many apps now failing to work on an older version of the iOS operating system.

Fig. 6.20 The task tracking app as installed on iOS 9. You need a valid Microsoft account to use it.

OneNote Online

OneNote Online

Like the Office applications this is the browser based version of the OneNote clipping and snipping tool that is used for storing and sharing information.

There is a desktop version of OneNote (Figure 6.21) and OneNote Online (Figure 6.22) displays all the stored information but the screen is laid out differently. The Desktop version is free to use and notebooks can be stored locally or in the cloud.

Fig. 6.21 OneNote on the desktop.

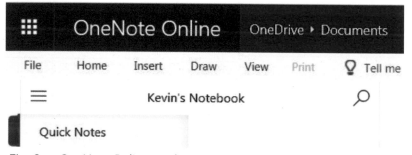

Fig. 6.22 OneNote Online in a browser or as an app is laid out differently to the desktop version for Windows.

Irrespective of the viewing method the notes and the clippings are stored in the same place and are accessible on all devices. Notebooks can be shared via e-mail with other people and they can edit or just view the contents. OneNote is available as an app on Android and iOS.

Sway

Sway

Sway is a visual design and editing application to create newsletters and brochures and many other eye-catching documents. The look and feel is similar to graphical web page designers and it can be used to create a blog. The results of your design efforts can be exported to Word or converted to a PDF document that is ideal for distribution.

There are none of the familiar Microsoft menu bars. Instead, you pick one of the document templates, choose a colour palate and style and add your content (Figures 6.23 & 6.24) and let yourself be guided by the in-built wizard.

If none of the templates and styles meet your needs then you can start from scratch and create your template.

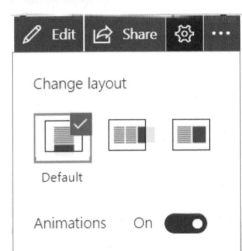

Fig. 6.23 Sway has many options to change the layout and the colour scheme of your newsletter.

Fig. 6.24 Sway prompts you to fill in essential information.

Flow

Flow is about workflow and automating tasks that you do on a regular basis. Flow is a form of coding and it has to be learned. Microsoft has a guided learning centre to help you.

Fig. 6.25The Templates section may have exactly what you need.

Save Office 365 email attachments to OneDrive for Business

Fig. 6.26 This flow strips attachments in Outlook and stores them in OneDrive.

When a new file is added in OneDrive, copy it to Google Drive and Dropbox

Fig. 6.27 I use this flow to make copies of my important images and photos automatically.

Not everyone wants to spend a lot of time working out how to get Flow to run, myself included, and the Microsoft team has provided a library of templates (Figure 6.25). You can search the Flow template library for your particular interests such as saving all email attachments (Figure 6.26).

The library has flows for several cloud storage providers and this is a clever way to have more than one copy of your data in the cloud. Of course you need an account with all the providers. Click on the image and the wizard launches to help you create and save your flow. The only downside I found is that the wizard does not let you create a new folder in your cloud accounts. I created the workflow shown in Figure 6.27 in about five minutes.

Sharing Documents

Fig. 6.28 Share a file or folder in OneDrive.

Fig. 6.29 A shared folder has this symbol.

You can share files and folders in your My OneDrive account by selecting the file and then Share (Figure 6.28). The share options are using email, a link and social media.

Once you share a folder it gets a people symbol attached to it (Figure 6.29). You can allow editing , set a password or an expiry date on the link.

The recipient gets an e-mail with a thumbnail list of the folder and its contents. Images can be viewed and downloaded and documents need to be downloaded before you can edit them.

Trying to edit online is confusing as you can go round in a circle trying to access the file that OneDrive has locked because you don't actually own it.   I hope Microsoft will iron out the file locking to make sharing a lot less frustrating. To stop the sharing click on **Share** once again and then **Manage Permissions** to find the Stop Sharing link for each person that has access.

Summary

OneDrive is a great personal product and the suite of apps will satisfy many of your needs. You don't need previous experience of using Microsoft Office to quickly learn how to create documents, spreadsheets and presentations. It is not a business grade system, probably designed that way given Microsoft's other premium products, even though you might get by using it for a while.

7

Microsoft Office 365

Office 365 is a subscription service that ensures you always have the most up-to-date software applications from Microsoft. There are Office 365 plans for home and personal use, as well as for small and midsized businesses, large enterprises, schools, and charities.

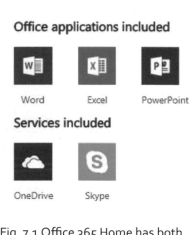

Office applications included

Word   Excel   PowerPoint

Services included

OneDrive   Skype

Fig. 7.1 Office 365 Home has both applications and services.

All Office 365 plans for **Home** and **Personal** use include the latest version of Microsoft Office, as fully installed applications. The office suite includes all the applications that you're familiar with, like Word, PowerPoint, and Excel, plus extra online storage, ongoing technical support at no extra cost, and more. You can pay for your subscription on a monthly or yearly basis, and the Office 365 Home (Figure 7.1) plan lets you share your subscription with up to four members of your household.

Most of the Office 365 plans for business, schools, and charities include the fully installed applications, but Microsoft also offers basic plans with the online versions of Office, file storage, and email. You can find out more about both family plans at **https:// products.office.com.**

Individuals do not have to buy their annual subscription from Microsoft itself and it is worth checking major online vendors for a one-off deal. For example, I bought my **Home** plan from Amazon at 33% discount for one year . The installation was very easy as the item had formatted a link that included the licence information.

Non-Subscription Version

Office 2016 is also sold as a *one-time purchase*, which means you pay a single, up-front cost to get Office applications for one computer. The software is yours to use for as long as you wish and many software packages are still available in that format.

One-time purchases are available for both PCs (such as Office Home & Student 2016) and Macs (such as Office Home & Student 2016 for Mac).

One-time purchases don't have an upgrade option, which means if you need to upgrade to the next major release, you'll usually have to buy the package again at full price. You will, however, receive security updates via the Windows Update Service.

Installing Office 365 Home

The installation process is well thought out and very clear to follow. The first step is to login with either an existing Microsoft account or by creating a new one as shown in Figure 7.2.

Fig. 7.2 You can use an existing Microsoft account or create a new one.

Hello. Let's get your Office

② Confirm account settings

Office 365 Home (1 year)

Country or region

United Kingdom ▾ ⑦

Your language

English ▾

Next

3 Get your Office

Fig. 7.3 Stage two may either ask for a 25 character product key or to confirm some basic information if the vendor passed the key automatically.

In Stage Two you have to enter a 25 character product key or if that was included in your download link from the online vendor you will instead be asked to confirm your location and subscription plan (Figure 7.3).

If you use your existing account the installation process will increase your OneDrive storage from 5GB to 1TB automatically. You will see this confirmed later in the installation process.

If you decide to end your subscription after a year Microsoft won't delete your files but you won't be able to add new files to OneDrive until you drop below the free limit of 5GB or whatever your new OneDrive limit is. You might decide to move back to Office Online and purchase 1TB of storage on OneDrive so that you have full editing rights again.

Office 365 Home

↓ Install
PC/Mac installs used: 0

Install Office on 5 PCs or Macs, 5 tablets, and 5 smartphones.

Install >

Fig. 7.4 The installation may take some time to complete.

Confirming your settings initiates Stage Three and a download of a setup file. Depending on the speed of the internet link and your home device it may take a while to complete Stage Three (Figure 7,4). The menu links and the messages you see are about the installation on the device you are working on.

The Office products install onto the PC or laptop in the background (Figure 7.5) and you may actually get error messages from Windows saying that the .exe, short for executable, file could harm your device.   Downloading the Office suite from a genuine Microsoft website will not harm your device. I'm sure Microsoft will correct this anomaly soon.

Installing Office

We'll be done in just a moment.

Fig. 7.5 The installation shows the office applications included in your subscription.

The installed apps are listed in the Windows Start menu and initially they have their full designation of Word 2016 but will soon revert to just Word, etc. The final message is about your new storage on OneDrive and any extras now included. The premium services include 60 minutes of calls on Skype, an account is required, a 50GB mailbox on Outlook.com plus 1TB of storage. Depending on your plan the benefits may be for a single or five users. There are full details on the Microsoft website that will usually be priced in your local currency.

Adding People

🧑‍🦱₊ Share Office 365
People shared with: 0

Each person you share with gets to install Office and gets their own additional OneDrive storage.

Share Office 365 >

Fig. 7.6 Sharing your Office 365 Home account with other users.

If you purchased Office 365 Home, as opposed to Office 365 Personal, you can share with up to five other members of your family (Figure 7.6). To add other people to your Home Office 365 account you need to go back to administration section of your Microsoft account and the Office 365 subscription should be listed under **Services and Subscriptions** (Figure 7.7).

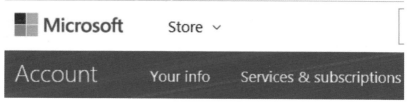

Fig. 7.7 Your personal account holds your Office 365 information.

As an individual using Office 365 access to the administration section is included in your personal Microsoft account. The Office 365 Portal available through links such as **https://login. microsoftonline.com** and **www.office.com** is to access Office 365 for Business and you will receive error messages using these links.

Sharing

To install Office each person needs their own Microsoft Office account and personal My Office Account page . They can create a new account when they accept the invitation you send them to share your subscription. People you share your subscription with get their own OneDrive storage but they can't access any files or folders in your OneDrive space unless you choose to share those files.

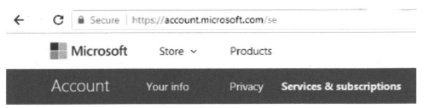

Fig. 7.8 Part of the Microsoft Account dashboard where the link to share your Office 365 Home edition is under Services and subscriptions.

Sharing Restrictions

If you don't see the **Sharing** link in your Services and Subscriptions you may not be the owner of the correct subscription (Figure 7.9).

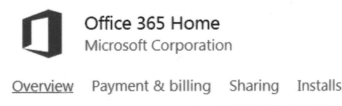

Fig. 7.9 The subscription owner will see these links but anyone you share with will not.

If you share with a family member they can't share onwards to another individual as shown in Figure 7.10.

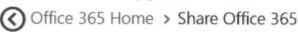

Fig. 7.10 Before you invite other people to use your subscription check the summary information on this pop-up window.

Once you share with another individual they can install it on more than one device, such as a tablet or phone. It is possible to deactivate an installation to free up that licence but the individual still has read-only access to their Office files.

They get to keep their extra OneDrive storage and can still access the install process if another licence comes free.

It is a bit extreme but if you are worried about another user then it may be better to cancel their subscription and then they lose all the benefits including the extra storage and revert back to a normal Microsoft account. Do warn them that their storage will drop from 1TB to 5GB even though they wont lose their files.

Sending Invitations

Login into the **Services and Subscriptions** section of your Microsoft account, click on **Sharing** and then **Manage Sharing** as shown in Figure 7.11.

 Office 365 Home

Overview   Payment & billing   <u>Sharing</u>   Installs

Total people who can use this subscription
5

Remaining people you can share with
3

    Manage sharing

Fig. 7.11 Your Office 365 Home summary shows how you have allocated your licences and a link to add other people.

ℛ₊ Share Office 365
People shared with: 1

Each person you share with gets to install Office and gets their own additional OneDrive storage.

> Share Office 365 >

Fig. 7.12 Access the invitation options by clicking on the Share Office 365 link.

Clicking on the **Share Office 365** button starts the invitation process. Next, click on **Add People** and then select one of the two options to send the invitation to your family member or work colleague. It is a bit long winded as you move from your account to the Office 365 portal.

Invitation Options

Sending the invitation via e-mail, Figure 7.13, is simple to do and the recipient receives an e-mail from Microsoft asking them to accept the offer to install Office 365.

Fig. 7.13 Option one is to e-mail the person directly with details of the subscription and a preformatted link to Office 365.

Alternatively, generate a link, Figure 7.14, that you can message to the recipient. Links do not expire and you have to delete unused ones manually.

Fig. 7.14 Option two is to obtain a link for inclusion in another document or sending via text message.

If they accept the invitation they repeat the steps shown in Fig. 7.2 to Fig. 7.5 on shown on pages 95 to 97. The installation process is similar on Windows 7 and Windows 10. The recipient may have to create their own Microsoft account to gain access to their 1TB storage on OneDrive. They do not share your storage. The process takes a while but it is simple to follow

Managing Office 365 Home

Here are a few insights on managing your account as we have covered most of the options already. When you login to your Office 365 account the opening screen (Fig. 7.15) is a little misleading as it just lists details of your own installation.

Install information

PC, Mac, and Windows tablet installs

Computer name   Installed

KPR-BUSINESS   17 February 2018
(Microsoft Windows 7 Professional)   Deactivate Install
Used By: You

Fig. 7.15 Install Information refers to your own installation.

To get more information click on **Share Office** and more options are available (Fig. 7.16). The entries we haven't seen before are **Manage People** and **Manage Invitations**.

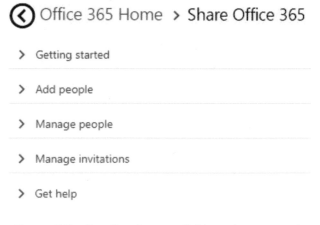

Office 365 Home › Share Office 365

> Getting started

> Add people

> Manage people

> Manage invitations

> Get help

Fig. 7.16 The list of options available to the owner of the Office 365 subscription.

Clicking on **Manage People** lists two people (Figure 7.17) sharing my subscription, myself included and I have options to **Stop Sharing** with this other person.

Fig. 7.17 My subscription is shared with one other person and there are three remaining spaces.

Manage Invitations (Figure 7.18) lists any manual links or e-mail invitations that remain unused and there are options to **Show** or **Delete** a link and **Resend** or **Delete** an e-mail invitation.

Fig. 7.18 Send new links in invitations or delete unused ones.

The other options are about your subscription, mostly around renewal and authorising Microsoft to do this automatically.

Check Your New Office 365

If you already had a version of Office on your PC or laptop you will probably want to check that you are using the newest version. The application may simply be called PowerPoint or Word without any other designation. There is a quick way to check its status.

Product Information

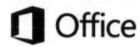

Subscription Product

Microsoft Office 365

This product contains

Manage Account

Fig. 7.19 This is clearly an Office 365 product.

Open one of your Office applications such as PowerPoint (2016) on your PC and click on **File** in the top menu and then **Account Information** to verify that you are using Office 365.

A few quick checks of the details under Product Information (Figure 7.19) should show that you are using the full version of that Office Online product. The key phrase to look for is **Subscription Product**.

One-time installs won't have any Account Information details.

Office 365 on Apple Mac

Office 365 for the Mac includes Word, Excel, PowerPoint, OneNote, Outlook, Skype and OneDrive. Publisher and Access are not available on this platform.

Android and iOS

Microsoft Office 365 is not available on Android or iOS. There are links in the Office 365 Home > Install section as shown in Figure 7.20.

If you follow the links shown by Microsoft you realise that you are installing **Office Online** that has apps available for both these systems.

Fig. 7.20 Office 365 Home has links to other devices but you can't install Office 365.

Office 365 Business

There are three versions of Office 365 for Business. They are **Business Essentials** that does not include Office but does have services like Skype, Teams, Outlook e-mail and the Yammer social network. **Business** includes Office and OneDrive but no e-mail and **Business Premium** includes everything.

Why do I need the Business Version?

The difference in using either Office 365 Home and Office 365 Business comes down to the intended use. The Home and Personal versions are for extended personal and family use. The Business editions are for commercial use, any business activities, basically any activity other than personal use.

Microsoft's licensing criteria are very complex and hard to understand. Rather than list the various options I will focus on the Home licence. Any activity outside this narrow definition requires a Business licence.

Home Edition Licence

Only one person at a time may use the software on each licensed device. The service/software may not be used for commercial, non-profit, or revenue-generating activities.

The components of the software are licensed as a single unit, and you may not separate or virtualize the components and install them on different devices. The licence is for direct use of the software only through the input mechanisms of the licensed device, such as a keyboard, mouse, or touchscreen.

It does not give permission for installation of the software on a server or for use by or through other devices connected to the server over an internal or external network. The software also is not licensed for commercial hosting. The use of servers and associated technology is beyond most user's abilities but IT people could exploit them.

Key Differences

Home* Plans	Business Plans
Comes with a fixed number of users,	Supports from 1 to 300 users. You buy as many as you need.
Users sign in using a Microsoft personal account.	Users sign in with a user ID known as a work or school account.
Simple administration of who gets to share the licence.	An administrator creates and manages user activities.
Email is accessed using a Microsoft account.	Email is stored in Office 365 and accessed via a user ID.
Files are stored in the OneDrive associated with a user's Microsoft account.	Files are stored in OneDrive for Business, a shared resource, and part of the user administration.

Fig. 7.21 The key differences between the Home (*also Personal and Student) plans and the Business plans.

The key message to take away from Figure 7.21 is that you need to appoint an administrator for the Business editions. If you are a sole trader then you end up administering yourself, which is not a problem in itself. There is a time issue because you have to learn how to configure your account, although for the most part the default settings will get you started.

The good news is that the Admin portal has links to training resources that you can work through at your own pace.

Switching from Home to Business

Having been made aware of the terms and conditions it is possible that you are using the wrong edition. You can get a refund in certain circumstances but they are very limited. Microsoft states that you may get a refund on a yearly subscription if you request it within 30 days of buying it. This is a very tight window and it is unclear what happens if you bought a plan through a third party.

Users on a monthly plan may not even bother with a refund as they simply cancel the subscription. You can request a refund within a 30-day window from your last renewal date

Your Microsoft account can have only one subscription associated with it. If you use the same Microsoft account to buy or redeem multiple Office 365 subscriptions, you will end up extending the amount of time your subscription is valid for **that** Microsoft account, not increasing the number of Office installs or amount of online storage you get.

The Business Editions

Each user can install Office 365 on up to five phones, five tablets, five PCs or five Macs and for that there is a 40% premium on the cost per user. Of course, you get access to 24/7 support and so considerable help with any issues.

The basic **Office 365 Business** plan looks like Office 365 Home, except it's licensed for commercial use, and up to 300 people can be added to the account at a cost per user. They are allowed to use the software on the up-to-five computers/tablets/phones per person. If you look carefully you will see that the Business edition does not include Publisher .

Office 365 Business Premium includes e-mail , with up to 50GB for email folders, that runs on resilient Exchange servers. There is also SharePoint for intranets and many other uses like document management, OneDrive for Business, Microsoft Teams to share information and Yammer to create your private social network.

You can host unlimited HD video conferencing meetings for up to 250 people with Skype for Business, let customers schedule appointments online with Microsoft Bookings, and manage tasks and teamwork with Microsoft Planner.

If you don't need the Microsoft Office applications but you do want enterprise-level email and SharePoint, you can go with **Office 365 Business Essentials**, which also includes OneDrive for Business, Skype for Business, Microsoft Teams, and Yammer.

With the E5 plan of Office 365 for Business, you get everything included in Premium, plus Microsoft Access, Power BI for business intelligence analytics, additional security features and compliance protection, Cloud-based call management, and PSTN conferencing to allow invitees to join Skype for Business meetings by dialling in from a landline or mobile phone. The 'E' plans are for large companies and I would recommend that you don't sign up for them.

Office 365 for Business is typically purchased through a Microsoft Partner but can also be purchased through some websites. You'll want to look at what each Office 365 for Business plan offers, because the cheapest (Essentials) is actually slightly less expensive than Office 365 Home, so using the Home plan isn't necessarily going to save you money.

The Premium Business Edition

Office applications included

Outlook	Word	Excel	PowerPoint	OneNote	Access (PC only)

Services included

Exchange	OneDrive	SharePoint	Skype	Microsoft Teams

Try Before You Buy

It can be a significant business expense to use Office 365 for Business and if you are not sure about its benefits then Microsoft lets you trial the Business premium edition for 30 days. The trial runs as a sub-domain on Microsoft's **.onmicrosoft.com domain.** Carry out a Google or Bing search and follow the Free Trial link. I recommend signing up directly with Microsoft.

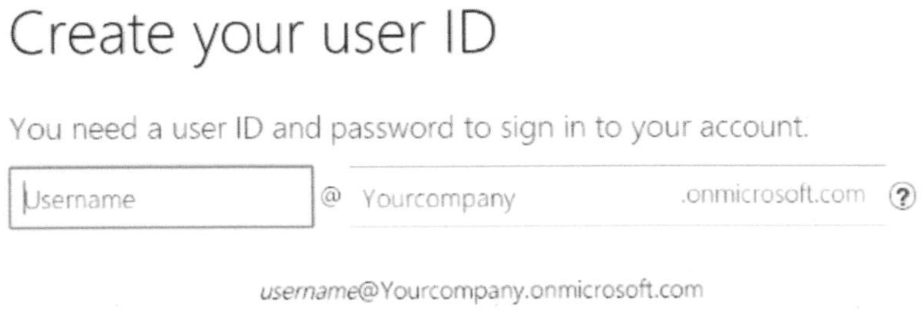

Create your user ID

You need a user ID and password to sign in to your account.

| Username | @ Yourcompany | .onmicrosoft.com ⑦ |

username@Yourcompany.onmicrosoft.com

Fig. 7.22 You can use your own domain later in the process.

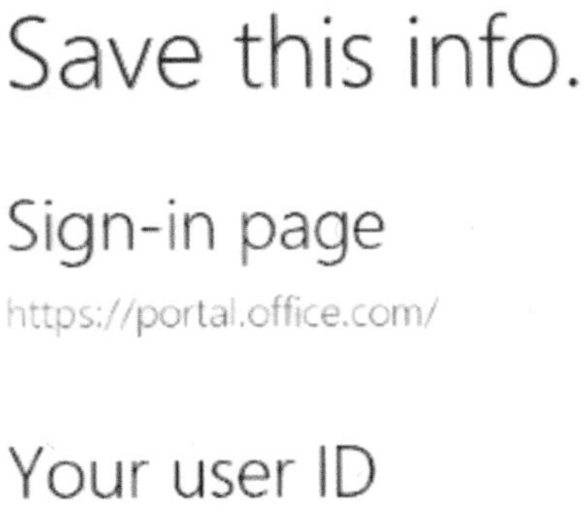

Save this info.

Sign-in page

https://portal.office.com/

Your user ID

Fig. 7.23 Make a note of the sign-in portal and your user ID and password.

The sign-up process is very straightforward apart from the format restrictions on names and passwords. You can pause the setup and complete it on another device. There are only a few questions about creating you User ID (Figure 7.22) that you are asked to note (Figure 7.23) along with the portal, **https://portal.office.com.**The process is in three stages. First, the main apps are installed on your device, then Exchange based email is setup and finally other apps are added in.

The estimated completion time is around 45 minutes but the process completed much faster than that. I experienced a few issues mainly because I realised that I didn't want the Business version on a particular device.

I exited and restarted the process on another device. A second complication was caused by there being an Office 365 Home user on the second device that confused me more than Microsoft.

Fig. 7.24 You get options to install the apps and services such as Skype for Business.

Figure 7.24 shows the installation of the main Office 365 apps and Skype for Business. There are two versions of Skype for Business. There is one version for Office 2016 on a PC and a 2015 version for the Apple Mac. Follow the screens and prompts through to the end. You can skip most steps and come back to them later.

Office 365 Admin

Fig. 7.25 Colour-coded status of the Office 365 setup.

The Admin Centre is a tidy dashboard that lists the configuration tools in a menu and summarizes the tasks you haven't completed (Figure 7.25) where I hadn't personalised my sign-in. To fix any issues click on **Go to setup** or get Microsoft Support to help you.

The Admin centre (Figure 7.26) on the dashboard is very clear and I suggest you look at billing (Figure 7.27) to make sure that you get ample notification of when the trial is nearing its end. If you miss the deadline then Microsoft just disables some functions. Microsoft will extend the trial for a further period but you will have to provide a credit card to bill against.

Fig. 7.26 Part of the Admin menu. Explore the various entries to learn about it.

Create at least one user (Figure 7.27) but note how many you create because you will be charged for each one if you move to a real subscription.

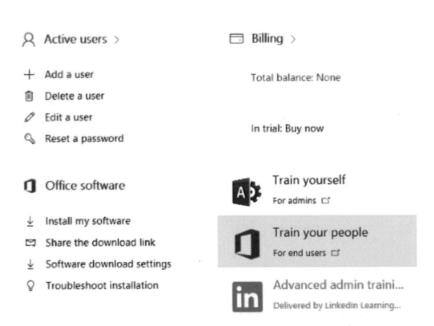

Fig 7.27 The other part of the Admin center including training resources.

Experience the training provided for the administrator and the users to make sure you and your team can work with this system. You must decide if the administration of it will take up too much time or uses technical concepts that you are not familiar with. It can be very easy to go wrong and undo a lot of hard work. Finally, login in as a user and create some documents.

Using Office 365 for Business

Office 365 for Business is aimed at businesses that have access to IT support specialists or someone very knowledgeable about servers and the internet. It has many advanced features in it that most smaller businesses won't need. These features tend to use a programming language called PowerShell. Like Google's G Suite you will have to set aside time to train someone to be an administrator.   You can get up and running quickly using the default settings for everything and simply add users (Figure 7.28). Users set themselves up mostly through a process called self-provisioning.

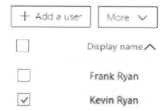

Fig. 7.28 For a quick start add users with default options.

There is a detailed PDF reference on the Office 365 support pages with a section on sharing the OneDrive for Business storage. Users start with a quota of 1GB that can be increased as needed.

Adding a Domain

In business you will want to have a domain that reflects your business. Microsoft prefers to use domains that you already own and if you have a domain you can use that to configure your online services. However, if you go to the Admin Centre and then to Domains you can buy a new domain reducing the chance of the new system damaging existing websites. Whichever option you choose just follow the instructions provided by Microsoft.

Collaboration

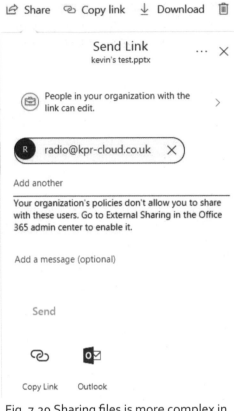

Fig. 7.29 Sharing files is more complex in OneDrive for Business where security is given high priority.

Office 365 for Business runs on OneDrive for Business that is very like the other versions. To share a document go to OneDrive, select Share. You will probably see a screen similar to Figure 7.29 about your organization's policies.

Office 365 has two types of external users defined as **Authenticated** and **Anonymous.** The former are users that have a subscription with any Office 365 product. They use Office Online to work on the documents you send to them. They can be added to the **Members Group** where they have more permissions to edit and create new documents.

When you share a file or folder with an authenticated external user, an email is sent to them which contains a link to the site or document. Each time they access the file or folder using the link, they are sent a time-sensitive code via email that they can use to verify their identity. They must enter the code to access the file or folder. You can stop sharing by deleting the sharing link that was sent to them or by setting the link to expire at a specific point in the future.

The latter, anonymous users, are not known to Office 365 and they can only view and edit the specific file or folders they have a link for. They can also share that link with as many people as they like until the link expires. To work with trusted partners Microsoft recommend that you use SharePoint to set up an external site or extranet to provide access to documents.

Admin Centres

Solving the problem of restricted external access can be a difficult task until you know that there are different systems within Office 365. Sometimes you need to change permissions in SharePoint and in other cases the setting is in OneDrive. Office 365 for Business is a big system and there is more information in Appendix 4 on **Yammer**, **SharePoint** and **Teams**. Being separate from Office 365, they merit their own admin centres as shown in Figure 7.30.

You can explore what each one does and by referring to Appendix 4 create some team sites using Yammer and SharePoint. These systems are now much simpler to setup than when they were first developed and are quite easy to use.

The ones to avoid are **Exchange** and **the Azure Active Directory** as they are geared to IT professionals. Be careful working in the Security and Compliance settings.

Fig. 7.30 Many other services have their own admin centres.

External sharing

Users can share with:

Fig. 7.31 The sliders control the permission levels for OneDrive and SharePoint. They work independently and the levels are very clear.

By opening the Admin Centre for OneDrive and choosing settings you find a single place to control external sharing for both SharePoint and OneDrive (Figure 7.31).   Getting this set up correctly is a time consuming task and I have found that links don't get delivered even when all the settings look correct and emails are delivered directly from Outlook.

Summary

Covering all the aspects of Office 365 for Business would take up the rest of this book. Once you understand where all the settings are, and this is a task in itself, you can make progress in setting up your internal users and external partners.

You can use it at what I would term a superficial level with Outlook email and maybe a SharePoint intranet. You soon find out just how vast the systems are and there is a learning curve for whoever the system administrator is.

8

Dropbox

Fig. 8.1 Dropbox offers plans for individuals and business.

Dropbox's focus is on secure storage with a few enhancements added in to the package. There is a free account with 2GB of space for personal use. You can earn more space by contributing to the community forum, completing the Dropbox tour and referrals to your friends. At maximum, you can accrue 32GB of extra storage. Dropbox almost hides their free account but you can get one by registering at **https://www.dropbox.com/register.**

Alternatively, you can upgrade your basic account to **Dropbox Plus** with 1TB of storage, offline access to your files and a camera upload option at around £8 per month on a rolling contract basis. Yearly contracts work out cheaper.

Fig. 8.2 Almost hidden away is the option to sign up for a new account.

My attempts to create an account on a PC failed for a reason that I could not identify and if that happens to you find and click on **Download the App** link that downloads a Windows installer.

Run the installer and when it completes you will see the login screen with some options (Figure 8.2). The **sign up** link will create your free account.

The next screen is to setup Dropbox on your PC (Figure 8.3).

Fig. 8.3 You can select the location of your Dropbox folder in your PC's directory.

The **Advanced Settings** let you change/select the location of the Dropbox folder. If you leave it the same as the location in Figure 8.3 the Dropbox folder will be grouped with OneDrive and Google Drive as shown in Figure 8.4. Dropbox provides a very short guide to how it operates. Anything you drop into the Dropbox folder on your device is copied to your account on www.dropbox.com.

The first time you view the files and folders in Dropbox you will find a ten-page guide to using it on many devices. You can download and print this guide. If you are new to cloud computing and cloud storage this is a good guide to how it works.

⭐ Favorites
◼ Desktop
🕙 Recent Places
⬇ Downloads
☁ OneDrive
📁 Google Drive
☳ Dropbox

Fig. 8.4 Dropbox with OneDrive and Google Drive.

Dropbox also installs an icon on the system tray on your PC or laptop. This is the portion of a standard Windows desktop that runs along the very bottom of the screen. It is their five diamonds logo in white rather than the blue version they use on their website.

Right click on this icon to open a status screen that has options along the top, part of which is shown in Figure 8.5

Fig. 8.5 Dropbox menu items.

Click on the gear wheel symbol to view or edit your preferences. The seven tabs are summarised in the table in Figure 8.6.

Tab	Important Functions
General	You can choose to show Dropbox as a save location in Microsoft Office. Will install an add-in to your Office Apps.
Account	Shows free space and an option to Unlink this Dropbox.
Import	Options to import photos and video, enable camera uploads or storage location for screenshots for the Print Screen key (PrtScn) on your keyboard.
Bandwidth	Defaults usually work well.
Proxies	Do not change unless you know what you are doing.
Notifications	Untick many of these once you have used Dropbox for a while.
Sync to Dropbox	Selective sync of folders on Dropbox to folders on your PC and option to move the location of the folder on your PC.

Fig. 8.6 Key settings to check in Dropbox on the PC.

Using Dropbox

Dropbox is now available as an extra storage area that is not on your PC or laptop. Sign in to Dropbox at https://www.dropbox.com using the user name and password that you created during the setup process and click on **Upload button** or the **Upload here** button as shown in Figure 8.7. The name can vary depending on your operating system. You can also drag and drop files into Dropbox. The files will be synced to all your devices for easy access.

> Upload
>
> ⚡ New shared folder
>
> ☐ New folder
>
> 👁 Show deleted files

Fig. 8.7 On Windows you are invited to Upload into a new folder.

Another common use of Dropbox is when you need to send a large file to someone that may be rejected by conventional e-mail systems as a too large attachment. Upload the file to Dropbox and **Share** a link with the recipients or **Copy link** to send to those that do not have an account.

You can collaborate on files together by creating a shared folder instead of e-mailing revisions back and forth to each other. You can create a shared folder when uploading or later.

Dropbox Paper

The basic account gives you access to **Dropbox Paper** that is an online whiteboard to assemble ideas or to take notes (Figure 8.8).

You need to verify your e-mail address before using it by clicking on the link sent to your email attached to this Dropbox account. There will be a file in your Dropbox account that is both a user guide and tutorial.

Fig. 8.8 Paper can be your online whiteboard.

is aimed at team working but individual users will also find uses for it such as making notes of a meeting, planning a project, organising meetings by linking Dropbox Paper to Outlook or Google calendars.

The Dropbox Paper app has it own home location at **https://paper.dropbox.com** where you will find more examples of documents as shown in Figure 8.9.   They are just skeletons or templates but give you some ideas of how Paper might be used.

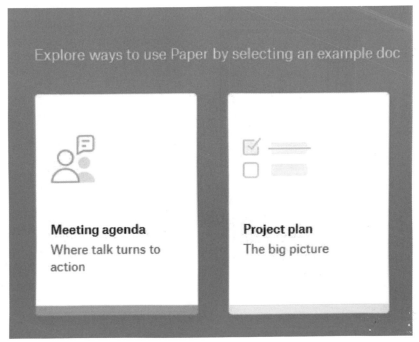

Fig. 8.9 Outline documents to get you started with Dropbox Paper.

Selective Sync

I found the help on this feature a little confusing. It is clear that documents on dropbox.com will be synced down to the PC. It is less clear how you can sync changes in an existing folder on your PC to your Dropbox account. I found this alternative method that puts you more in control of the process.

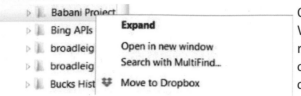

Fig. 8.10 Move folders to Dropbox.

On your PC open Windows Explorer right click on a file or folder and the option to **Expand** gives you an option to **Move to Dropbox** (Figure 8.10). This action moves the folder from its current location, creates a folder of the same name in Dropbox and syncs the content back to your PC. The folders seem unchanged but they have been moved to Dropbox that has put a set of shortcuts in their place.

Breaking Sync Paths

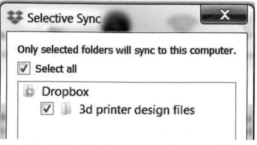

Fig. 8.11 Selective Sync controls in Dropbox.

In the Sync section of your preferences you can opt to update folders synced to your device by unticking them (Figure 8.11). You get to your preferences by clicking on the Dropbox icon on the system tray. Doing this will remove the shortcuts that I mentioned above from your PC, but they are still on dropbox.com.

To get them back either download them from Dropbox or reverse your action in the preferences by ticking the boxes in the Preferences section once more. There may be a few minutes when they seem to have disappeared but Dropbox will update itself.

Other cloud storage providers do exactly the same thing and this process of moving your data from your local device to the cloud is the essence of cloud computing. If it makes you nervous then ensure that you create other physical backups of your data.

Dropbox Help

Each section has guides accessed using the question mark icon. There is a central help function at https://www.dropbox.com/help if you have other questions.

Dropbox and Microsoft Office

Microsoft Office add-in

☐ Show Dropbox as a save location in Microsoft Office

Fig. 8.12 Tick the box to load the Dropbox add-in into Microsoft Office.

In the Preferences section there is a tick-box as shown in Figure 8.12. You will have to restart Office for it to appear. The My Places bar disappeared with Windows 7 when it was replaced with a Windows Explorer view.

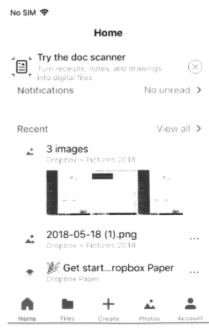

Fig. 8.13 Dropbox on iOS.

Dropbox for iOS

There is a Dropbox storage app for iOS. Do not install the EMM version which is for large businesses. Part of the desktop is shown in Figure 8.13. The layout is very different to the PC desktop version. The first thing to notice is that the app has a **doc scanner** for receipts, notes and drawings. The Paper for Dropbox app provides access to the whiteboard. You should be able to install Paper if you have already set it up on another device and the **Example Docs** folder is still in the **Files** area of your Dropbox account.

Android

There is a Dropbox app that is slightly different to the iOS one that I found easier to use in landscape mode. It has a direct link to Paper for Dropbox but no reference to the doc scanner on the home page. The scanner or **Scan Document** appears as one of the options to add a new file to your storage area along with creating a simple **Text File**.

Offline Files

Both Android and iOS have options to make individual files available offline. You find the option in the settings, three horizontal dots, for each file. This option is not available on a PC desktop in Windows 7 or Windows 10 where you can download a copy of the file to your laptop or Microsoft Surface to work on it offline.

Plans for Individuals

Dropbox has two paid plans for individuals called **Plus** and **Professional**. Both plans provide 1TB of storage but there are some differences to justify the £10 difference in monthly cost. The Plus plan costs around £7 per month with a yearly payment. The data security is the same in both, but the Professional provides 120 days of file recovery against the 30 days in the Plus plan. Both plans provide integration with Microsoft Office 365.

Dropbox for Business

Dropbox for Business or for Teams offers more storage starting at 2TB of shared space for **Standard** users and unlimited space for **Advanced** users. The business plans introduce more user control and administration across all Dropbox applications and devices using Dropbox apps and require a higher level of IT knowledge to operate it.

Smart Sync

Smart Sync is a Dropbox feature that helps you save space on your hard drive. Access every file and folder in your Dropbox account from your computer, using virtually no hard drive space. Smart Sync Is available for Dropbox Professional customers, and members of Dropbox Business teams. You can work down at the individual file level.

Sharing

Fig. 8.14 Sharing files and folders is straightforward.

To share a file or folder login to your Dropbox account and hover over the item to reveal the Share button. Click on this to send a sharing link (Figure 8.14) to the recipient who has to join Dropbox.

Summary

Dropbox's negative feature is the small amount of storage provided in their basic or free account. At just 2GB you quickly use that up. Of course, you may like Dropbox and Dropbox Paper enough to buy a plan. The other aspect that needs improvement is the inclusion of a simple office suite to work within your account.

9
Box

Box is another well known name in the cloud storage business and has additional applications to make in more attractive to users. Box (Figure 9.1) advertises a free account with 10GB of storage.

Signing up for this account is straightforward and finishes with a confirmation e-mail that requires a response to verify the sign-up. The URL is **https://www.box.com**.

Once you are logged into your new account you can choose to personalise your account for private or work use and send and share e-mails with others. You can skip through all this but you will have to scroll through the short introductory guide and it is worth doing this to understand what makes Box different to the other storage providers.

Fig. 9.1 Box offers simple, secure file-sharing from anywhere.

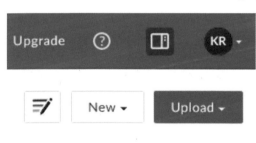

Fig. 9.2 Box controls normally appear on the top left of your browser screen.

Your Box desktop should now be open (Figure 9.2) and providing you with a menu on the left hand side and a lot of whitespace where lists of files would be. Your account is empty at this stage.

Check your **Account Settings** to make sure you are on the correct time zone and your sharing settings.

Box   9

Get Box Sync now

Work from your desktop while
keeping files in sync.

Fig. 9.3 Download the sync tool if
you plan to

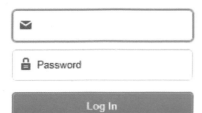

Fig. 9.4 The simple Box login
screen.

Check the other tabs as you
might find items like **Profile,
Security** and **Diagnostics** useful
in the future.

Box Sync

Install this software if you plan to
automatically sync files between
your PC and Box (Figure 9.3). The
installation completes without
user intervention but then you
have to log back into Box to
complete the setup (Figure 9.4).
There should be a Box icon in the
system tray on your PC or laptop

Box Sync is still installing at this
point and in the installation
window click on Start Syncing to
launch Box on your desktop.
Windows Explorer will create a
Box Sync folder under
Favourites. Box works by syncing
content from Box.com to your
device. You can upload content
from your PC and the files will
appear in the Box Sync folder.

Box Apps

Box has its own app store like
Google Play and Apple. A few
apps are already available in the
storage area and clicking on the
New button on your Box desktop
opens a list of file types that you
can work with.

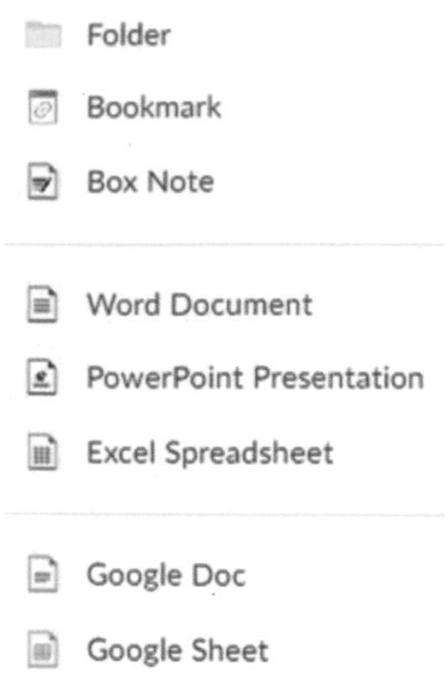

Folder

Bookmark

Box Note

Word Document

PowerPoint Presentation

Excel Spreadsheet

Google Doc

Google Sheet

Fig. 9.5 Create files in Office Online and Google formats.

The available file formats are shown in Figure 9.5. The document is created directly in your box.com desktop.

The Box app store has both official and third party apps. The official store is located **https://app.box.com/apps.**

Figure 9.6 lists some of the filters available to reduce the list by your operating system (platform), function (what you want to do) and by the cost.

My Applications

Official Box Apps

Platform

Mac   Windows

Function

Collaboration   Printing

Content   Project
Management   Management

Cost

Free   Premium

Paid

Fig. 9.6 Some of the categories available.

Click on **My Applications** link as shown in Figure 9.6 to get a list of the pre-installed apps. There will be some applications that you do not recognize and these can be deleted.

There is an CAD, Computer Aided Design, viewer from Autodesk that is widely used in the construction industry and two digital signature applications.

Box Edit

This lets you edit files in your Box account using the software installed on your Window computer.

Box   9

The instructions on getting this to work are not very clear and you may have to read a number of support articles on the community forum. Box Edit needs you to install Box Tools first of all. Follow the links to the Box Tools help page and then the downloads link page at **https://www.box.com/en-gb/resources/downloads**. The link is titled **Box Edit for Windows** and clicking on this link downloads the **BoxToolsInstaller.exe** Run the installer and follow any instructions on the screen.

Fig. 9.7 Word Document uploaded from a PC may have two default apps listed to read and edit them.

Box Edit has a slightly odd feature but in a way it is logical. It will only open the document in your online account with an installed piece of software if the document was created with that software.

Figure 9.7 lists three documents with Test Test.docx highlighted. This document was created with Word 2010 and Box offers to open it with either Microsoft Word, because it was installed on my PC or Word Online. The document called Box Training was created directly in Box using Word Online and that will be the only option provided.

Box Notes

Box Notes (Figure 9.8) lets you create notes that you can share with others. It works with Mac and Windows. It is a separate download available after you login to your account.

Fig. 9.8 Box notes is aimed at business.

Box Notes has six templates for you to use. They are **Blank**, **Meeting Agenda**, **Calendar**, **Project Plan**, **Project Status** and **Newsletter**. You can create your own note using the simple editor. The note can be **Shared** with other Box users or via an e-mail link.

Box Capture

Capture helps mobile workers quickly snap photos, videos or document scans and then upload them securely to your Box account. Box Capture is available on iOS but not Android.

Box Drive

Fig. 9.9 Box Drive integrates the cloud with your desktop

Box Drive (Figure 9.9) is a another download that Box describes as a simple way to stream all of your files (even terabytes of data) right to your desktop.

However, there are issues in running both Box Sync and Box Drive on the same machine and Box Notes will be opened by the most recently installed or updated product. If you need access to files offline then you need to use Box Sync. Also, Box Drive is not compatible with all the anti-virus security software and results in un-expected results.

Other Box Software

Box Relay is a workflow app, similar in concept to Microsoft's Flow to automate and standardise procedures in a business. **Box Skills** is an advanced search tool using Artificial Intelligence. This is a development project only available to customers on the Enterprise plan. **Box Shuttle** is a simple link to choose your Box storage plan.

Box   9

Sharing Your Box Account

You can share files and folders by selecting the **Share** option (Figure 9.10) that provides a link or a place to enter e-mail addresses (Figure 9.11). The three dots symbol opens options to update or rename a file. The gear wheel provides options (Figure 9.11) to add a password, set an expiry date, stop recipients downloading the file and create a custom URL that makes more sense than the Box generated one.

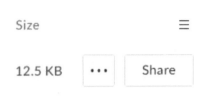

Size   ≡

12.5 KB   •••   Share

Fig. 9.10 Click on the three dots to set options for individual files.

Shared link for Test Test.docx

Shared link   ⚙

https://app.box.com/s/4jtkz6gfmanms6mpipq9rpk2nc   Copy

Anyone with the link can view and download this file.

Fig. 9. 11 Click on the gear wheel to set secure file access.

Mobile Versions

The basic Box app is available for both iOS and Android. Box Capture is available on iOS. Both Box app versions have an offline files facility.

Summary

Box uses Microsoft Office Online to edit files with its cloud store. Add in a free plan with 10GB of storage and simple interfaces makes Box is a serious alternative to OneDrive and Google Drive.

10

Apple and iCloud

Apple's cloud storage service is called iCloud and is used for backups of your Apple devices, transfer of device settings to a new device, storing documents and photos, saving passwords and to locate a lost or stolen iPhone or iPad. If you own Apple devices you'll already have iCloud pre-installed and usually all you need to do is turn it on by accessing your settings.

Fig. 10.1 iCloud for Windows is best downloaded from Apple's website.

However, if you have mixed devices then you might want to take advantage of iCloud on your PC (Figure 10.1). Android does not have any official apps and I haven't found any third party ones that I would recommend for use with iCloud. There are several in the Google Play store that claim they are compatible with iCloud and will sync calendars, contacts and reminders but the feedback ratings are not very high.

The restrictions are imposed by Apple that in general blocks the synchronization of photos and files from apps that do not meet Apple's strict quality tests.

iCloud for Windows

You should download iCloud for Windows directly from the Apple website **(https://support.apple.com/en-gb/HT204283)** where there is more information on the product. This is a large 153MB download. It should install easily on Windows 7 but you can have errors installing it on Windows 10. The Apple support website has a number of articles on how to fix these installation errors.

The installer puts an icon in the notification area of the Windows desktop and clicking this icon gives you access to iCloud Photos and ICloud Drive. You have to enable features in iCloud and you do this through Settings. Right click on the Apple iCloud icon in your system tray and then click on **Open iCloud Settings** to configure the features you wish to use (Figure 10.2).

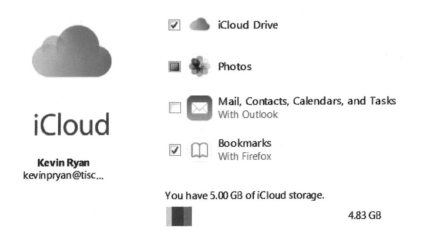

Fig. 10.2 The iCloud Settings interface for Windows. It is a mini dashboard detailing the storage usage on iCloud Drive.

Photos on Your PC

Apple has the **iCloud Photo Library** to store and make available to

PC users images and videos captured on your iPhone or iPad. The **iCloud Photo Sharing** service controls who has access to this media. Clicking on the

Fig. 10.3 Click on Options to tell iCloud how to handle your photos.

Options button (Figure 10.3) gives a list of options controlled by tick boxes to enable the features plus a **Change** button (Figure 10.4) to add in specific folders that iCloud can use.

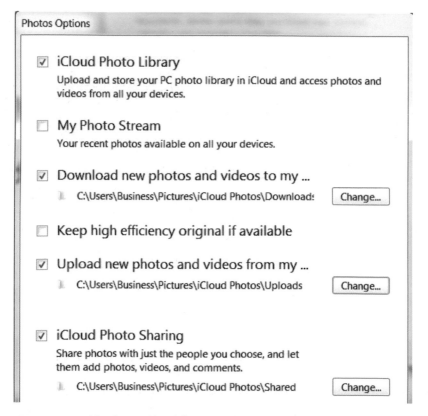

Fig. 10.4 Enable those iCloud features that you want to use.

Manage Cloud Storage (PC)

iCloud provides 5GB of free storage and when you login from your PC there is a colour coded bar (Figure 10.5) detailing how much space is taken up by photos and videos, backups from Apple devices, documents and mail. Click on the Storage button (Figure 10.5) to get more information on how the storage is being used (Figure 10.6).

You have 5.00 GB of iCloud storage.

    4.83 GB   Storage

Fig. 10.5 Hover over the coloured bar for a detailed view.

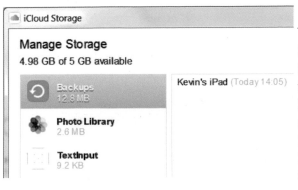

The installer adds **iCloud Drive** and **iCloud Photos** to the list of folders in Favourite Places as shown in Figure 10.7. In Windows 10 check under Quick Access.

Fig. 10.6 Backups from my iPad Mini use just 12.8 Mb of storage.

There will be empty upload and download sub-folders in the iCloud Photos folder. If iCloud Drive is missing from Windows Explorer go back to the Settings options and tick iCloud Drive to make the shortcut appear. If you still have problems check for an answer on the Apple support website.

⭐ Favorites

▬ Desktop

🗐 Recent Places

🗐 Downloads

🌸 iCloud Photos

☁ iCloud Drive

Fig. 10.7 iCloud shortcuts are added to Windows Explorer.

iCloud Drive on iOS

If you use an iPad or iPhone with a version of the operating system at iOS 9 or lower you may need to update your settings to display the iCloud icon on your screen. Enable iCloud drive, choose your options for Photos and Bookmark sharing between Safari and the other major browsers and enable Mail Contacts, Calendars and Tasks if you require it.

Photo Apps on iOS

If you haven't accessed the Photos app on your Apple device for a while you may get a message asking you to update to the newer version called the **iCloud Photo Library.**

iOS 11 Changes

Apple made a significant change to iCloud Drive with the release of iOS 11. The familiar iCloud Drive app was replaced by the Files app (Figure 10.8).

Fig. 10.8 The iOS 11 Files app uses the familiar folder icon.

In the new Files app, shown in Figure 10.9, your iCloud Drive is listed as a location. The app has list and folder views, and lets you sort by name, date, size, and tags.

If more cloud apps are installed they are listed under More Locations. Tap to see which ones they are as shown in Figure 10.10 on page 137. Tap or slide the button to add this to the available list of locations that hold files. Files supports many providers including OneDrive, Dropbox, Google, Adobe Creative Cloud and Box.

Locations

☁ iCloud Drive

▢ On My iPad

⋯ More Locations   ❶

Fig. 10.9 iCloud is now a location.

Locations

Fig. 10.10 OneDrive is available but not enabled. Slide the button to green to enable this location.

To see the files in iCloud just tap on the link and you will see the files and folders stored in the Documents partition on the iCloud Drive.

If you have the associated app, such as Microsoft Word installed on you iPad then iOS will use it to open the document.

If not then you will see options at the top of the screen that include an editing pencil (Figure 10.11).

Clicking on this icon opens up the document that has editing tools down the left hand side of the screen next to the text.

iWork Apps Folders

Fig. 10.11 If there is no installed app iCloud opens a default editor.

If you use the Apple iWork suite of apps, alternatives to the Microsoft and Google ones then you will notice that they have their own folders on iCloud Drive. The iWork apps are Keynote for presentations, Numbers to work with spreadsheets and Pages to create documents.

Numbers

Backups

iCloud backup makes a copy of the information on your iPhone, iPad and iPod touch. When your device is backed up in iCloud, you can easily set up a new device or restore information on the one you already have. iCloud automatically backs up your iOS device information daily over Wi-Fi when your device is turned on, locked, and connected to a power source. In your device's settings you can configure automatic and manual backups.

If you want to check what is actually being backed up open iCloud in Settings and tap on **Manage Storage**. Depending on your version of iOS you will see the information shown in Figure 10.12 although some of it may be in a different place on the screen. The apps that are being backed up have sliders next to them and you can exclude them from the backup by sliding the button to the left so that the

Fig. 10.12 Connect to iCloud to check the status of your backups and to configure the apps that are being backed up.

green colour disappears.

If you wish you can disable the backup process completely although you can see why this is not a good idea.

Restore from Backup

As the name suggests this process restores content and stored data such as app settings, home-screen layouts, etc. Saved account login information is restored if the backup was encrypted. Apple's backup philosophy, and they are not alone in this view, is that a cloud restore recovers a factory reset device or configures a new device so that it operates like the original. Files, and Photos are not copied as you should have been storing these in the cloud.

This is a complex topic and I recommend that you search the Apple support website to get detailed instructions for your particular device.

iCloud Drive Apps

Apple created applications for documents (Pages), spreadsheets (Number) and presentations (Keynotes) and named them collectively as iWork (Figure 10.13). The apps are available for Windows by logging into your iCloud account with your browser. On iOS the apps are on the App store but you will need a recent version of iOS, the current or previous major release to run them. You have to **get** and **install** the three apps from the App Store.

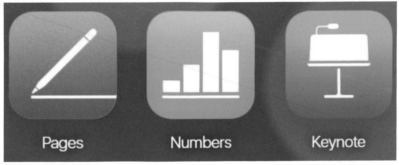

Fig. 10.13 Apple's apps that you can use instead of the Microsoft or Google alternatives.

Pages

Login into your iCloud account and from the list of available apps chose Pages and start by choosing a simple template such as Blank. Pages is a no frills word processor with **text options** to style the various sections of a document, miscellaneous fonts, character alignment for paragraphs,   line spacing, bullets and lists and indents.

There are **section options** for page settings such as headers and footers and numbering. The **document options** set page size, margins and orientation.

As shown in Figure 10.14 Pages supports tables, graphs, text boxes, shapes and images (jpeg, png and gif) and adding comments to text.

Blank

Fig. 10.14 The simple menu bar but there are other text options in a sidebar.

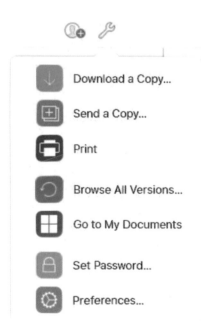

Download a Copy...

Send a Copy...

Print

Browse All Versions...

Go to My Documents

Set Password...

Preferences...

Fig.10.15 The tools menu has a download option.

The tools menu , shown in Figure 10.15 has options to download your work in four formats. They are Pages, Word, PDF and EPUB for electronic publications. To upload documents from your PC choose **Go to My Documents** (Figure 10.15) and upload the document into **iCloud Pages**. Note that this area is separate to **iCloud Drive.**

Pages converts Word documents to its internal format for editing. To go back to Word format use the **Download a Copy** option. Advanced formatting may be lost or altered during these conversions.

Sending documents requires a functioning iCloud Mail . Mail can only be set up from an iOS or a macOS device.

Pages Preferences

Each document can have preferences shown is Figure 10.16. The General Settings relate to the author name and to enable spellchecking. The Guides Settings is shown in Figure 10.17.

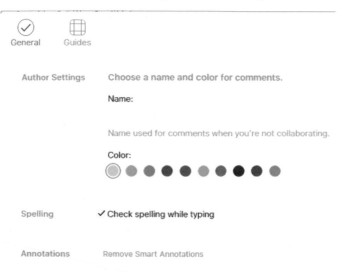

Fig. 10.16 The General page preferences are basic and the Guides position images or other objects on a page.

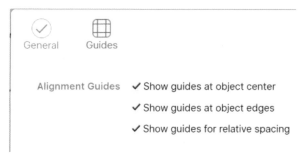

Fig. 10.17 Pages provides three guides to lay your document out neatly.

Collaboration

Sharing of documents is restricted to Apple and Windows users.

Add People

Add people to this document, then send them the link.

Add: | kevin@kpr-web.co.uk ∨ |

> Share Options   Only people you invite can make changes

Kevin Ryan (kevinpryan@tiscali.co.uk)   Cancel   **Share**

Fig. 10.18 Start sharing your document or check who already has access to it.

Collaboration works on a restricted number of devices that Apple updates from time to time. Search the Apple support pages to keep up-to-date. The 2018 list is below.

♦ A Mac with macOS Sierra and Pages 7.0, Numbers 5.0 or Keynote 8.0 or later.

♦ An iPhone, iPad or iPod touch with iOS 11 and Pages 4.0, Numbers 4.0 or Keynote 4.0 or later.

♦ A Mac with Safari 9 or later, or Google Chrome 50 or later.

♦ A Windows PC with IE 11 or later, or Google Chrome 50 or later.

You can invite other people to collaborate in two ways. If your colleagues use iCloud or iCloud.com , and you know their apple IDs (e-mail addresses) they can login and work on the document in their own Pages area. If you send people a link they will be invited to login with their Apple ID or create one if they are not registered.

Fig. 10.19

Figure 10.18 shows the process of adding people after you click on the Person icon on the editing toolbar (Figure 10.19).

Numbers

Doc 3 Results 2015

Fig. 10.20 There is a standard toolbar in the three iWork apps.

Numbers, the spreadsheet app has a similar screen layout to Pages with a simple tool bar above your spreadsheet shown in Figure 10.20. Once you click in a cell or other active area of your spreadsheet more options open in a sidebar (Figure 10.21).

Numbers deals with Excel .xls and .xlsx formats but I had trouble uploading .csv files. This could be an issue because

Fig. 10.21 The cell options. Uploaded files have some changes blocked.

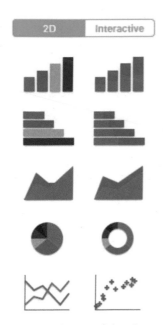

Fig. 10.22 Some of the chart options in Numbers.

converting these files to .xls before uploading cloud can add formatting that causes data corruption in database tables.

Charts

Numbers creates the usual 2D charts and interactive charts (Figure 10.22) where you can add sliders to show how data changes over time. If you import a 3D chart into Numbers for iCloud it will convert it to 2D but retain the 3D information.

You can create 3D charts in Numbers on iOS and macOS but once the worksheet is saved to iCloud it will show as a 2D chart in a browser.

Keynote

 Animations aren't fully supported in Internet Explorer.

Fig. 10.23 A warning using IE 11 on Windows 7.

Fig. 10.24 Open the options by clicking on the slide itself. Here are some of the options to format the slide's title.

I found that Keynote for iCloud worked best with the Google Chrome browser on a PC. Internet Explorer 11 was a close second but I did lose some functionality (Figure 10.23). Using the apps on either iOS or macOS should be trouble free.

You can learn how to use Keynote in a reasonable amount of time especially if you are familiar with PowerPoint (Figure 10.24).

Again, there are differences in using Keynote for iCloud and the app on an Apple device. It is easier to amend your slide's layout on iOS or macOS.

Collaboration, i.e. updating a set of Keynote slides works reasonably quickly with changes on one device appearing on another in under a minute.

Other Apps

Fig. 10.25 Other iWork apps that are useful

Summary

What's New in Numbers

New Chart Options
Adjust shadows, backgrounds, and gaps.

Rounded Corners
Give charts a new look with rounded corners on columns and bars.

New Shapes
Enhance your spreadsheets with a variety of new editable shapes.

Fig. 10.26 New features added to Numbers primarily in visual effects.

The Apple office suite may seem very basic and not give you the features you need. The apps get updated regularly (Figure 10.26). Bear in mind that Apple is competing against Office Online and Google Docs and not the full power of Office 365. Apple uses Microsoft formats for file interchange and if you own a lot of Apple hardware then use IWork until you outgrow it.

11

Citrix

There are other suppliers of cloud services, you will find them using an internet search engine, but most of them are aimed at big business. One of the few that might work for a small business is provided by Citrix. Citrix is well known to IT professionals especially for their secure remote access to company servers.

Citrix ShareFile

Citrix markets their ShareFile (Figure 11.1) service as the meeting

ShareFile

Fig. 11.1 Citrix is trusted in the world of secure products.

of business-class file sharing and real time collaboration. Google's G Suite could claim to do the same thing but Citrix has added other security features that meet several industry standards. These legal and financial standards might have features that you considered valuable or even critical for your particular business.

Citrix's entry level Personal Plan with 100 GB of storage costs around £160 p.a. billing annually or £200 p.a. billing monthly. Citrix's pricing is in US dollars so these are typical prices for the Personal Plan that will vary with the exchange rate. However, this entry level plan only allows you to create one employee. In addition to the administrator. Find out more information and current pricing at **https://www.sharefile.com**.

Customer Branding

The appearance of your ShareFile portal can be changed to be a better match with your own website. You can add your company logo, background image and select a primary colour, although the colour palette is limited.

As far as your customers or clients are concerned they are logging into your portal to access their files and not Citrix. You make the changes in the Admin part of your dashboard and the options are easy to choose. There is no coding involved.

ShareFile Trial

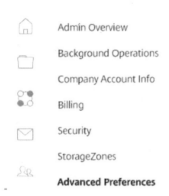

There is a lot of information on the ShareFile website but it is tightly written in a technical format. Citrix provides a 30-day trial of its Business Plan so you can experience all its features. You sign up in a few minutes without any financial commitment.

There is an option in the **Billing** section of the **Admin Settings** of the dashboard (Figure 11.2) to cancel the trial at any time.

Fig. 11.2 Part of the ShareFile dashboard.

Security Options

ShareFile is a great system if your business needs to send or provide secure access to files for clients, vendors, customers and others outside your company. You can also give those same people permission to use certain features in your account. With ShareFile, you can share files and folders with as many people as you want at no additional charge.

Citrix refers to **Multi-Factor Authentication** where you use your phone or another device to provide an extra layer of security for new device logins. Other vendors refer to this as two-factor authentication.

Available for both client and employee users, this feature sends a verification code via text message (SMS) or voice call after you enter your password to ensure that only you can access your account, even if your password has been compromised.

There are other security features that you can enable. You can lockout an account after a predetermined number of attempts to login and you can set the duration of the lockout. There is also the choice to make that user re-authenticate themselves. Another option lets you block IP addresses if you can identify that login attempts are coming from a particular IP.

Mobile Apps

Request With ShareFile

Request items securely by using the ShareFile messaging system.

Fig. 11.3 Users of the iOS and Android apps can request access to a file.

Citrix ShareFile has mobile apps, available for all iOS, Android, Windows and Blackberry devices. You get seamless access to all the files, folders and some other features of your account on the go.

I found that you cannot get full administrator access through the app and you will have to login to your account using a browser like Chrome. You can browse, send, request files (Figure 11.3) or set folder permissions, that means adding or deleting users.

You can edit Microsoft Office files or annotate PDFs in ShareFile and create new documents.

iOS Apps

There are two ShareFile apps in the Apple App Store. The first accesses your ShareFile storage and works well. The ShareFile Workflows app is complicated to set up because you have to generate custom forms in the Admin section of your account. ShareFile does not list it in the administrator dashboard under the apps for mobile devices and I recommend that you ignore it.

ShareFile for iOS and Android

The iOS and Android apps are very similar in look and feel and have the same functionality. The apps let you edit existing files and create new ones in .docx, .xlsx and .pptx formats. The ShareFile app may use another app already installed on your device to open a document or use the default content app in ShareFile (Figure 11.4) if it can't detect one.

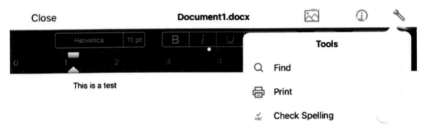

Fig. 11.4 The ShareFile document editor with some options.

The ShareFile content app creates documents, spreadsheets and presentations. The app is not as developed as Office Online or Google Docs. Files created using one of the three ShareFile native apps can be opened with a compatible app on your device (Figure 11.5) if you prefer using it.

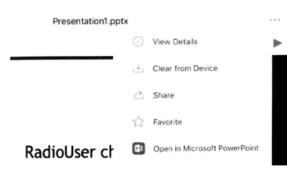

Fig. 11.5 You can open files created in ShareFile with a compatible app on your device.

If two apps are installed then both will be listed when you open a file and the choice is then yours. You may not use the content app very often but it is a good way to quickly create a document.

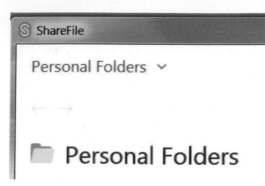

Desktop App for Windows

The ShareFile Desktop App (Figure 11.6) for Windows PCs, laptops and mobile Windows devices such as the Microsoft Surface lets you upload, download, send and request files from your desktop. This app gives you access to your personal folders and the File Box shared

Fig. 11.6 The Windows desktop app may be useful in certain circumstances although using a browser provides much more functionality.

file repository. The desktop app uses any software installed on your device to edit your files and make them available offline.

Versioning

Fig. 11.7 Version tracking and control is a useful feature.

File versioning lets you keep and view every single previous version of a file (Figure 11.7) when a new one is uploaded with the same name. With this feature, any files with the same name automatically save as the latest version, with the option to view earlier versions.

Use this feature for documents put into a complicated workflow where a sequence of multiple edits and added comments would otherwise cause confusion.

Other File Controls

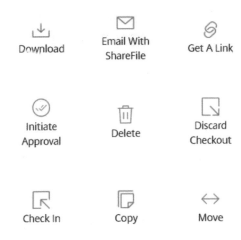

Fig. 11.8 ShareFile has several options to control access to files and to send them to recipients.

Figure 11.8 shows the available controls for a file. Some like **Download** and **Copy** are obvious. **Emailing** is restricted to people in your address book. Otherwise you need to add them as a client. Files can be locked for editing by you using the **Check-In** feature and released by **Discard Checkout**. If customers are working on the file they may get confusing error messages and lose access to particular file versions.

Digital Signatures

Citrix's Team Plan has a feature where you can send files stored in your ShareFile account to others for secure, legally binding electronic signature. Once signed, documents are saved automatically back to ShareFile, so you never have to follow up with clients or chase down documents again.

Encrypted Email

When securing just the attachments on your email isn't enough, ShareFile allows you to encrypt the body of your message to your recipient as well. It's a simpler way to support compliance and add security and the recipients don't need a username or password or have to be ShareFile customers to view or respond to an encrypted email. This is only available in some plans.

Workflows

If your business has to get someone else to approve, comment on, or suggest changes to a document, or agree to a purchase order, then you can route that document to one or more individuals for sign-off. There are no   email threads and you can send notifications and reminders and set deadlines.

Tracking Approvals

Fig. 11. 9 Every document in an approval workflow has a summary of the actions attached to it.

There is a detailed list of annotations and activity on every document in workflow (Figure 11.9) visible in the ShareFile dashboard and attached to the document received by all the recipients. If a recipient is not responding, holding up the process, you can skip them. Mobile users receive instant notification and the document is released to all authorised users.

Summary

Citrix ShareFile is about security and getting documents to recipients in a secure way. These document trails can be audited and the system itself meets many international standards. ShareFile is not an office suite but it is a very secure file store and file transfer application for businesses that need high security.

12
Amazon

Amazon Prime is well known to users of the Amazon website and we probably associate it most with free delivery of goods. Amazon Prime includes an app called **Amazon Photos** and associated with that is **Amazon Drive** for general storage of documents (Fig. 12.1).

Fig. 12.1 The two parts of the Amazon cloud service

If you want to use Amazon's free storage then the first step on Windows devices is to download the setup file and run it. Start the process from this URL: **https://www.amazon.co.uk/clouddrive.** You need an Amazon account (Figure 12.2) to get and install the software.

Welcome to Amazon Drive

Fig. 12. 2 You need an Amazon account to set up Amazon Drive.

Once installed the app immediately asks you to backup photos and videos to Amazon Drive but you can leave this until later or not do it at all.

The Amazon Drive interface allows you to pause or cancel the backup at any time especially if you realize just how much you are uploading over your internet connection.

Introducing Backup

A simpler way to secure your files and photos online

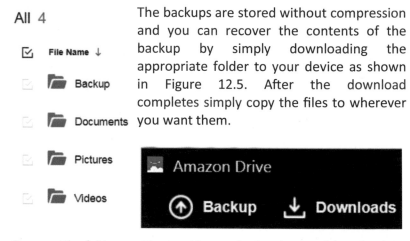

☑ My Pictures
1316 items

☑ My Videos
1 item

If you cancel the backup you are taken back to the start screen shown in Figure 12.3 where you can select a different folder.

The backup should complete without errors and by skipping through any remaining introductory screens you get a view of your storage on Amazon Drive as shown in Figure 12.4 These are the default folders.

Fig 12.3 The entry point to Amazon Backup.

All 4

☑ File Name ↓

☐ 📁 Backup

☐ 📁 Documents

☐ 📁 Pictures

☐ 📁 Videos

The backups are stored without compression and you can recover the contents of the backup by simply downloading the appropriate folder to your device as shown in Figure 12.5. After the download completes simply copy the files to wherever you want them.

🖼 Amazon Drive

⬆ Backup   ↓ Downloads

Fig. 12.4 The folders in Amazon Drive.

Fig. 12.5 You can both upload and download your files on Amazon Drive.

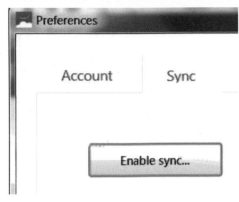

Fig. 12.6 One click enables the backup function in Amazon Drive.

By default the Amazon app does not create a virtual drive on your Windows device. To create the drive you must enable the Sync options in the preferences as shown in Figure 12.6. Note that enabling Sync causes the app to restart so make sure that you are not in the middle of a backup. Sync has options to choose folders (Figure 12.7) on both the drive and on your local PC.

☑ **Enable sync for your Amazon Drive**

Amazon Drive folders: Choose folders...

Local sync folder: Select folder...

C:\Users\Business\Amazon Sy...

Fig. 12.7 You have control over which folders to use to sync your files.

Storage Plans

The free plan is a generous 5GB but not an exceptional amount of storage and 100GB is available for around £17 per annum. Amazon Prime subscribers have **unlimited photo storage** included in their monthly subscription but don't get any extra document storage. Other plans are available up to 30TB of storage but are expensive. Check whether the other major providers are offering a better deal.

Accessing Amazon Drive

Access Amazon Drive using **https://www.amazon.co.uk/clouddrive** and login with your Amazon user ID and password. You will login to your familiar Amazon store area. Amazon Drive will be listed on **Your Account** dropdown menu.

Understanding File Storage

You can move files around by either dragging and dropping them into your Amazon Drive via the browser interface or using Windows Explorer to cut/copy and paste them. The files will be added as new items to Amazon Drive and will appear under All Files. If they are in the wrong place then by selecting the file or folder you can either Move to Trash or Move to another folder such as Documents as shown in Figure 12.8.

Fig. 12.8 Move files to another folder or move them to you trash folder.

The changes take a little time to happen which can be confusing when you use Amazon Drive for the first time. Moving files and folders into the Documents folder on Amazon Drive has the effect of deleting them from the folder named Amazon Drive on your PC.

Fig. 12.9 Other options in Amazon Drive to share, rename and download files.

Note that if you do certain things like renaming (Figure 12.9) a file or folder before the move process completes then the file or folder may still appear on your local drive with the original name.

Like every system you need to spend a little time working with files and folders that you could afford to lose should you make a mistake. Amazon Drive is better than many others at leaving you in control of local deletions.

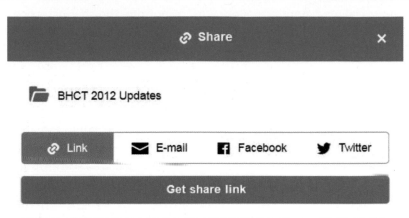

Fig. 12.10 The share options include social media as well as e-mail.

Sharing Documents

Desktop Email ⌄

Desktop Email

Gmail

Yahoo

Outlook web

Hotmail

AOL mail

Fig. 12.11 Amazon supports a few e-mail providers but not all the common ones.

Amazon has four share options (Figure 12.10) including two for social media. The easiest is **Link** that provides a URL to use in documents or an e-mail. You simply copy and paste the link that lets the recipient download and/or view the item.

E-mail has options for a number of desktop e-mail clients, Figure 12.11, or you can just use the local default of Desktop Email. This is a bit misleading as the option is for you to select which client to use on your PC.

Amazon will open a new e-mail window with the link and add some standard text for you to edit. Complete the e-mail and send it as normal. This is one of those actions that you can over think.

The social media options allow you to continue the sharing process using your Facebook or Twitter accounts. Shared files and folders are listed under Shared on your Amazon Drive dashboard.

Android App

The Amazon Drive app is available on the Google Play store for installation on your tablet or Android mobile phone. The display of information is uncluttered and there are options to display items as tiles or a simple list with thumbnails. The interface is very similar to the one for iOS shown in Figure 12.12.

iOS App

Apple iTunes and the App Store has the Amazon Drive app for installation on iPads and iPhones. The display of the folders is uncluttered and there are options to upload other files from your device and create new folders as shown in Figure 12.12. Amazon Drive has viewers for most common file formats.

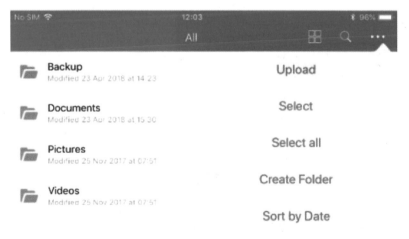

Fig. 12.12 The Amazon Drive app on iOS with a view of your folders and options to create or upload a new folder.

Amazon S3

Amazon Web Service's (AWS) Simple Storage Service (S3) is available to use for free for a year but there are aspects of it that expire after a year. It is a complicated suite of services squarely aimed at big businesses that have access to IT developers. It is a pay as you use system that might be attractive in certain niche areas of activity. I include it in this book for completeness as I believe that it is just too complicated for the individual or small businesses to use.

Common Uses of AWS

The AWS Solutions web page lists many of the ways you can use Amazon S3 and I have summarized some of those activities below.

Backup and Storage provides data backup and storage services for others. **Application Hosting** provides services that deploy, install, and manage web applications. **Media Hosting** to build a redundant, scalable, and highly available infrastructure that hosts video, photo, or music uploads and downloads. **Software Delivery** for your software applications that customers can download.

The Free Tier

The AWS Free Tier splits into five areas but the one of most interest for small businesses is probably **storage and content delivery**. The others are computing power, database development and business analytics. By all means, take advantage of their free trial offer but I found the start-up documentation too time consuming too digest.

Summary

Amazon is not the first provider you think of when considering cloud storage. Amazon doesn't really promote it. The backup app is probably the simplest one to set up and use. AWS S3 is a big business tool that is too onerous to setup for a small business

13

Hosted Office 365

Many of the website hosting companies offer combinations of Microsoft Office 365. They are aimed at business but you can available of them for personal use. Business packages have good technical support and have better reliability.

Fig. 13.1 The main Office 365 applications.

The various apps are offered in three combination usually called Business Essentials, Business and Business Premium. All three are aimed at small businesses. There are three other Enterprise packages aimed at larger organisations that I include for reference.

The Business Essentials is usually Outlook e-mail on an Exchange e-mail server plus Skype and OneDrive for Business. You will probably get 1TB of storage and OneDrive has Office Online built-in. Not all vendors show OneDrive or Skype but look for storage capacity and video conferencing. You may also get access to Teams, SharePoint, One Note and Yammer. There is more information on these applications in Appendix 4.

The Business package includes the main Microsoft applications (Figure 13.1) without Skype and no hosted e-mail service. The Outlook app is included. The Premium service is a combination of these two packages. The two higher level options let you install the Office 365 package on up to five devices provided these devices are used by the same person. If you have five people in your organisation then you need five licences.

All the packages run on Windows devices. Publisher 2016 is not available for the Mac and those Apple users who want Skype for Business will have to make do with the older Lync for Mac 2011.

Choosing a Provider

There are many providers selling access to Office 365 and not all offerings are the same. Read the online information carefully as you may be paying for using Office Online rather than Office 365. Discounted prices usually mean that you are signing up for a whole year.

Using Hosted Services

Figure 13.2 Provider 1&1 has packages with just Exchange email.

Most of the well known internet services providers offer various packages of Office 365 services. 1&1 (Figure 13.2) starts with Exchange based e-mail using the Outlook web client. The next tier adds in Skype and a 1 TB OneDrive for Business and the top tier adds in Office 365.

Other providers such as Fasthosts, GoDaddy and 123 offer very similar packages and some include a free UK domain(.uk, .co.uk, etc.) for a year to establish your business presence. With Microsoft Exchange you get more than just e-mail because through it you can set up calendars and contacts, invite people to meetings and see if they are available before sending out invitations.

Using a third party is an alternative to using the products direct from Microsoft itself. Typically, the third party providers will be a little cheaper than Microsoft, but not always. Once you remember that any package that includes only OneDrive for Business means you will be using Office Online and not Office 365 you will likely find a good deal if you shop around.

14

Other Services in the Cloud

Companies are adding their niche services to the cloud all the time and it is worth checking if software you currently use is now available as a cloud service.

In this chapter I will give you an overview of the business areas where there are now established companies offering their well-known products as a cloud service.

Accounting

Intuit Quickbooks

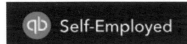

Home

Transactions

Fig. 14.1 The self-employed edition may be all you need.

I used Quickbooks desktop for many years when I ran a limited company even though the small business edition on the desktop had many functions that I never used. My accountant was happy to accept a data export from the software so that they could prepare my annual accounts.

Once I changed to being self-employed this software package was too much of an overhead and I moved to Microsoft Excel and a simple invoicing package.

With a move to the cloud Intuit has online plans for businesses and the self employed (Figure 14.1) who can now have the essential features they need for around £100 per annum. The self-employed dashboard is clear and well laid out. There are separate windows for Profit and Loss, Expenses, Accounts, Invoices, Mileage

Add your first transaction

Use spreadsheets? This is way easier. Enter
details from a recent business expense. Add
notes or attach a receipt, if you like.

	DATE ▼	TRANSACTION

Fig. 14.2 Add transaction and any notes to
understand the entry later on.

and Estimated Tax. Here you can add transactions (Figure 14.2),
input receipts and mileage, generate invoices and an estimate of
taxes due. However, it may not do everything you need if you are
both in a job and also growing a business of your own.

We're mobile too!

Expenses, mileage, and
receipts—all on your phone.

Get the app

Fig. 14.3 Quickbooks sends a link to your mobile device.

There are apps for iOS and Android (Figure 14.3) so that you can
log details and raise invoices on the go. This feature is not unique
to Quickbooks and there are other providers available. There are
other Quickbooks apps in the Apple and Google stores but they
are associated with the Essentials and Plus plans used to manage
employees, VAT and payroll.

Sage

Sage is perhaps the other best known company in the small business world. There are other businesses with the word Sage in their trading name. Sage is at **https://uk.sageone.com**.

Sage doesn't have the equivalent of Quickbooks self-employed pricing plan. It is squarely aimed at the small and medium business sector.

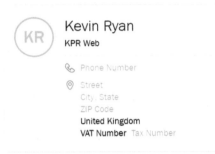

Fig. 14.4 FreshBooks has clear US roots branded for the UK market.

FreshBooks

FreshBooks (Figure 14.4) is a US based company that is an alternative to Quickbooks but is more expensive. It splits customers into Creatives & Marketing, Legal and Consultancy, Trades and Home Services and IT & Development. There are sub-categories to choose from and questions on how mature your business is.

Fig.14.5 Some of the menu items.

The main menu (Figure 14.5), configured in response to my business choice of a Web Service. In **Estimates** you can create proposals online, customise them and add an e-Signature that locks the contents of the proposal. The **Projects** and **Time Tracking** sections are linked and in the latter you can record hours spent by clicking on a timeline and adding some extra details. You can choose not to bill for the work. There is much more in the package and FreshBooks offers 30-day trials.

Each section has online videos to help you learn how to set up and add your data to each section.

FreshBooks has connectors to all the major UK banks and supports connections to many others including credit card providers. FreshBooks integrates with PayPal.

Wave UK

Fig. 14.6 Wave provides 100% free software.

There are many other online accounting packages available for use. Wave (**www.waveapps.com**) is an alternative to a paid for cloud service. Wave (Figure 14.6) configures your service slightly depending on which broad industry segment you select.

Figure 14.7 shows part of the main menu with the Sales entry expanded. There are menus for **Purchases, Accounting, Banking, Payroll** and **Reports**.

A big selling point is that Wave accepts payment via credit cards using the Stripe payments processor. There is a cost per transaction for doing this.

Wave is probably a good fit for a small business that deals directly with the public at craft and food fairs. For freelancers and those self employed people who are tied into projects it includes Estimates but lacks time tracking and projects where charging time to a particular customer is essential.

> ⦿ **KPR Web** ›
>
> ⊙ Dashboard
>
> ▭ **Sales** ⌃
>
> Estimates
>
> Invoices
>
> Recurring Invoices
>
> Credit Card Payments
>
> Customer Statements
>
> Customers
>
> Products & Services

Fig. 14.7 Part of the main menu in the Wave cloud service.

Desktop Publishing

Desktop publishing covers a wide field of interest and you can create very nice newsletters using Microsoft's Sway and to a lesser extent with Google Slides. You might find an Add-on for Google Drive such as Lucidpress but bear in mind my recommendation of a cautious approach when installing any of these add-ons.

If you are creating something for physical printing and are doing this as part of a team then there are only a few vendors that could be classified as being a cloud-base service.

Adobe Creative Cloud

Adobe offers plans for individuals, students and teachers, business and places of learning. Each plan gives access to a number of Adobe apps. The Photography plan at £120 per annum is the cheapest plan with options for Lightroom CC plus 1TB of storage or Lightroom, Photoshop and 20GB of storage.

2D Drawing

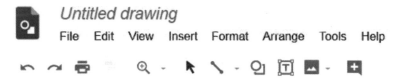

Fig. 14.8 Google has a Drawing tool hidden away in Google Docs

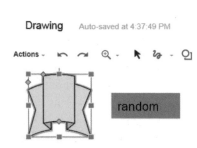

Fig.14.9 A shape and text box.

Google Docs has a drawing tool in its dropdown menu in Google Docs that opens in a new window (Figure 14.8). It is also available in Slides and Sheets. The version that is included in Google Docs is very slightly different (Figure 14.9) to the one found by searching on the web.

3D Drawing

 **SketchUp**

The easiest way to draw in 3D, now in a web browser.

Fig. 14.10 SketchUp in a browser.

Google invented SketchUp (Figure 14.10) that is now a separate app that is great for 3D modelling. It recently moved to the cloud using a browser to create your drawings.

SketchUp is used by 3D printer enthusiasts to create models and convert the shape to command files to send to the printer for rendering. It is a complex package and takes a lot of use to get the hang of it but there is an instructor mode (Figure 14.11)

Fig. 14.11 The instructor is a tutorial on using the tools to create entities.

There are warehouses of components, materials and styles to help you create your entity as fast as possible. Your finished model can be turned and viewed from a number of angles that SketchUp calls perspectives as shown in Figure 14.12.

The Free package has 10GB of storage and access to the 3D Warehouse that holds finished models. Up to five people can collaborate on your projects but you can't turn your ideas into real things. To create something physical requires an upgrade to SketchUp Shop at around £100 per annum or you need to subscribe to the more expensive Pro version.

Fig. 14.12 Choose a viewing angle.

Appendix 1

Gmail in an Email Client

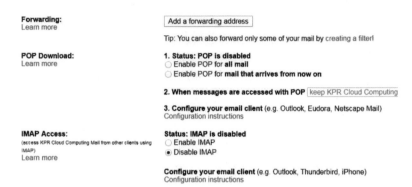

Fig. 15.1 Under the Forwarding and POP/IMAP you need to enable either POP downloads or an IMAP connection.

You may want to use your own e-mail client to have Gmail or your email accounts managed by Gmail alongside any other email account you need to check regularly. If you are just using Gmail then you will find all the settings by logging into **www.google.com/gmail** with your Google account. You will have to enable either POP or IMAP access on your account (Figure 15.1) in your settings in Gmail.

These settings must match those in your desktop client. Look at your e-mail account's properties and check they match those on the Servers tab in Figure 15.2.

Fig. 15.2 The server tab in your e-mail client needs to access the Gmail incoming mail server.

Fig. 15.3 Each type of mail server has designated
port number .

On the Security Tab check that you are using the correct port
numbers as shown in Figure 15.3.

Gmail in G Suite

If Gmail was provided as part of a G Suite plan there are other
global settings that you access by drilling down in the Gmail entry
in the Google Apps list. Here you can enable/disable POP and IMAP
for all users, enable a connection to Microsoft Outlook, enable the
Gmail plugin for Chrome users, manage spam email settings and
create a whitelist of approved email addresses that bypass the
spam filters and enable message scanning when spam levels
increase.

Appendix 2

G Suite Admin

The administration of G Suite is beyond the scope of this book and the essential elements are listed below. I have not covered Admin Roles or Device Management.

Dashboard

The dashboard has **Insights** that are warnings or actions for you to review. You will be reminded to assign admin rights to another user or verify your e-mail address

Users

This is where you add, remove and manage your users and create Organisational Units to mirror your business structure.

Billing

Check the plan you are on and any upgrades available to you or cancel your subscription. Set up bank or credit card to pay your subscription and view your monthly bills in detail.

Reports

Reports track the usage of all the services available in G Suite. There are reports on apps, user activity, mobile devices and there is a separate section on auditing.

Apps

The top level view shows how many G Suite apps, additional Google services, marketplace apps and security apps are available. Drill down in the G Suite apps to control who has access to each one.

Groups

Use this tool to create groups and mailing lists, Add and manage users, group access to apps and services and assign aliases if needed for a short term project.

Security

There are various settings including monitoring password strength by user and setting up user authorisation for web based apps like Gmail and Calendar. You may have to change settings to fix security warnings.

Domains

Add or remove domains you own and are linked to G Suite or give them an alias to match your branding. Each domain or sub-domain added has to be verified.

Data migration

This tool has to be run three times to import email, contacts and calendar data. It may not work with your current email client. G Suite has a list of email clients that work with this tool.

Appendix 3

Move e-mail to G Suite

Go to the control panel for your domain

Delete existing MX records.

Create new MX records for G Suite.

Save the MX records

Fig. 15.4 Some of the options in G Suite to control the mail DNS records.

Fig. 15.5 cPanel's DNS Zone Editor.

If do choose to move your e-mail handling to Google follow the steps in the GSuite setup as shown in Figure 15.4.

There are details of or many hosting companies but you may be like me and find that your host is not there. In addition, you may find that your host won't accept some of Google's suggested settings. If you have no idea how to access your control panel (Figure 15.5 and Figure 15.6) then re-consider moving your e-mail to Google's Gmail servers.

Zone Records for "kpr-cloud.co.uk"

| Filter by name | | | | | | Q | + Add Record ▾ |

Filter: All   A   AAAA   CAA   CNAME   MX   SRV   TXT

Name	TTL	Class	Type
kpr-cloud.co.uk.	14400	IN	MX

Fig. 15.6 A detailed view of the DNS records including MX.

It may be worth searching your host's online knowledgebase as they may have included instructions there. Once you have the instructions on how to access cPanel login, find the DNS Zone Editor. Once in the editor ensure your are editing the **MX, Mail eXchanger** records.

Priority	Name | Host | Alias	Value | Destination
1	@	ASPMX.L.GOOGLE.COM
5	@	ALT1.ASPMX.L.GOOGLE.COM
6	@	ALT2.ASPMX.L.GOOGLE.COM
10	@	ALT3.ASPMX.L.GOOGLE.COM
10	@	ALT4.ASPMX.L.GOOGLE.COM

Fig. 15.7 G Suite provides five records to replace those setup by your hosting provider.

 Verify your domain and set up email

Email setup complete. Verifying domain...

About 50 minutes left...

Fig. 15.8 The timer is only a rough indication of the time to complete.

Make a note of the entry you are about to delete in case you need to go back. Delete the existing entries and use Add Record to add the five records Google lists (Figure 15.7). Accept your host's defaults for Name, TTL and Priority. You have now finished the setup process and verifying your domain and e-mail will probably take a lot less than 50 minutes (Figure 15.8). The change from one mail provider to another can take two to three days but usually it will change in much less time than that. Figure 15.6 on page 172 shows that the Google servers that I use for my DNS with the new entries. If you still use the DNS settings from your ISP then the full changeover can take much longer.

Appendix 4

Microsoft SharePoint

Communication Site

Choose a design

> Topic

Use this design if you have a lot of information to share such as
news, events, and other content.

Fig. 15.9 A template for a communications intranet.

SharePoint is usually used for document management , a process
for businesses to name, share and store their documents in a
structured way. It is also used for intranets, a private internet
controlled by the business. Another use is to extend that intranet
outside the business as an extranet. Office 365 has a wizard to
create your intranet site and offers several templates (Figure
15.9).

The SharePoint design interface is easier to use than in previous
versions. Outlook also connects to SharePoint and adds an
Outlook Customer (OC) intranet site. There is a separate Admin
Centre for SharePoint to configure security and to assign users
various permissions to add and edit documents.

Yammer

Yammer is a social media platform for use within a business that can be used for whatever topics a business allows. There may be a section for work activity like projects and a section for private use like personal adverts and the promotion of events. You can make staff aware of all this by referring them to the **Yammer Usage Policy** that you will find under **Network Admin** in the Yammer settings. There is also a general Microsoft privacy policy on user pages. You can add a company logo , manage users and set a data retention policy.

GETTING STARTED

20%

Write your first post

Follow your coworkers

Start a Group

Get the Yammer Mobile App

INVITE YOUR COWORKERS

Yammer works best when your team is here too.

Invite them now

Fig. 15.10 Suggested actions for a Yammer user. Admin has other actions to set up the Yammer network.

Yammer is set up using a wizard and Figure 15.10 shows the four activities you need to complete to get started. Of course, you need to invite your co-workers to contribute.

Yammer has one click features such as sending a **Poll** out , **Praising** a colleague who did great work and sending out an **Announcement**. Yammer support private messaging as well.

Teams

Microsoft Teams is a crossover product that mirrors features found in other products and pulls them together in one place. It aims to create a collaborative workspace where team members communicate publically or in private channels that can be organised by topic.

Communication can be text based or by using the built-in video conferencing and screen sharing that allows online meetings. This could be a useful tool for customer support or ad-hoc training.

DR Digital Radio Testing > General ···

Conversations   Files   Wiki ∨   +

Fig. 15.11 Teams has extra options indicated by the + sign and the three horizontal dots.

Teams has many options collected in sub-menus at several points on your Teams desktop (Figure 15.11). The plus (+) sign usually means that you can extend a set of visible tabs by adding other apps from various providers (Figure 15.12).

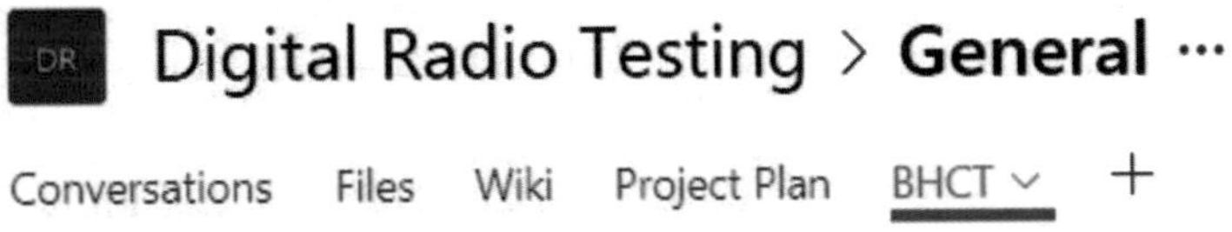

DR Digital Radio Testing > General ···

Conversations   Files   Wiki   Project Plan   BHCT ∨   +

Fig. 15.12 Two extra tabs added to include Planner (Project Plan) and a Website (BHCT). Websites must start with https:// to be valid.

Teams is a portal where resources from many sources both inside Office 365 and outside it can be assembled as a desktop. You can work online or download the desktop app for Windows.

Appendix 5

Google Sites

Google Sites is part of G Suite and is not available in Google Docs. Google sites does a similar job to Microsoft SharePoint and you can use it for internal team sites. Google created a newer system, **New Sites** that is part of Google Drive for Business, and refers to the previous version **Classic Sites,** part of the G Suite Admin Console. Anyone in the G Suite system can be given permission to create a website.

Using Google Sites

INSERT   PAGES   THEMES

Tᴛ

Text box

◪

Images

You can access Sites directly or form within your G Suite Admin Console. You can choose Classic or New Sites. Click on the Create link to being the process and then use the menu (Figure 15.13) to insert objects from Google Drive or from social media.

< >

Embed

☁

Upload

Components   ⌄ ⌃

—   Divider

Fig. 15.13 The website is created like a document.

You website (Figure 15.14) is like a document and you need to share it with other people. Either widely to anyone who can find it or by inviting specific people. You can restrict what the recipients can do by way of changing the content.

Untitled Site

🖪 Opened 3:22 PM

⋮

Fig. 15.14 a New site.

Index

Index